HERSTORY:
BLACK FEMALE RITES OF PASSAGE

by Mary C. Lewis

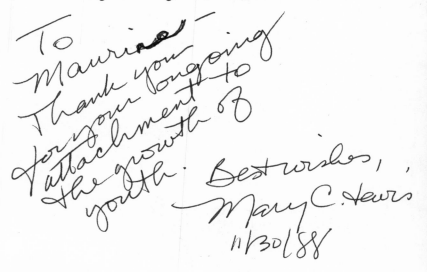

To Maurice —
Thank you
for your ongoing
attachment to
the growth of
youth. Best wishes,,
Mary C. Lewis
11/30/88

AFRICAN AMERICAN IMAGES
Chicago, Illinois

Cover Illustration by Yaounde Olu
William Hall/Photo Credits

First Edition
First Printing

Table of Contents

FOREWORD

"Why, I feel so tall within—I feel as if the power of a nation is within me!"

—Sojourner Truth, 1878

Over one hundred years ago, when Sojourner Truth spoke about feeling "tall," I am certain she was talking about much more than physical height. Indeed, in the same breath she also used the words "power" and "nation." By connecting these three terms, our heroine of the ages has given us a range of possibilities to embrace—a forest to be cultivated within and around us. Essentially, this book is meant to examine the possibilities of growth for Black females.

The image of a tall, powerful nation, a "forest," so to speak, is applicable for what has always been needed from Black women. Whenever I think of any Black heroines—famous ones as well as those within my own family—I always picture those for whom courage, strength, resourcefulness, and abiding faith have been a daily part of their existence. No matter how little appreciation was given or how much society mistreated our female forebears, they have always provided the nurturing for our growth as a people.

Nowadays, what are the possibilities of growth when it comes to our "saplings"? I am speaking now about Black adolescent females, the young who are moving rapidly toward womanhood. I can hardly call them "teenagers" because many of them are still preteens. Nevertheless, they are proceeding speedily; their environment, complete with its blaring, multi-faceted messages of aggressive sex appeal, material wealth, and uncontrolled violence, demands that they become women NOW—or yesterday, if we are to believe the rate at which our society tells everyone to behave. Indeed, for far too many of our young, it would seem that adolescence is not a time of possibilities but a time in which possibilities are taken away.

So what can be done to make sure Black adolescent females possess a broad range of possibilities for their growth? This book is meant to provide access to what is conceivable for our soon-to-be-women. Therefore, the biggest goal of this book is to expand your thinking about Black females—what it means to be one and what it might mean to become an adult one.

Hopefully, the book will also enlarge your definition of adolescence. When I began working on this book, I thought I knew what adolescence meant. I was quickly humbled; not only was I forced to admit my ignorance, I soon realized that many specialists are similarly uncertain. It doesn't take a so-called expert, though, to recognize that adolescence holds no single meaning; in fact, it is a period of complex and varied elements, some physical, some emotional, some biological, some psychological, some social, some cultural—none of which, when singled out, can total adolescence. That is why Chapter One, "Her Many Developing Selves," provides a backdrop of information about the physical, intellectual, social, emotional and cultural identities being formed during a young Black female's adolescence.

Adolescence, for many of us, is by far the most puzzling period of life. No matter how much "book learning" anyone gains, as any parent or teacher will testify, when it comes to the adolescent years, we more or less throw up our hands in despair. Mood swings, rebelliousness, preoccupation with self, breakdowns in communication, and all the "outside" dangers of drug use, gangs, pregnancy, and peer pressure—you name it, parents are forced to confront these and other issues during their child's adolescent years. Far too often, the confrontations are like mismatched battles—somehow the parent gets the feeling that she or he doesn't have nearly enough ammunition to win.

In addition, during adolescence, the very nature of self-identity is called into question. This means, for our young "saplings," that issues related to Blackness inevitably surface. What, you might be asking, don't they already know what it means to be Black? Without seeming to be a know-it-all, I believe most don't know yet. Most of our young people, male and female, are still struggling with a definition of

Blackness—understandably so. For in their struggle is *our* struggle to reach a common definition that welcomes the rich diversity we possess and banishes forever the abusive stereotypes that were never ours to begin with.

Adolescent Black girls must also wonder what being and becoming female is all about. They must because they are driven to some extent by biology—the approach and onset of fertility. But they are influenced by social needs too. In their push for acceptance by their peers and their relatives, they seek to feel certain of their femaleness—but just what does that include? And what does that exclude? What does it take to be a woman by today's standards? Are there any rules to go by, or does anything go? Although many young females may not ask those questions directly, they are asking them indirectly by their behavior, their dress, and their attitudes toward each other and toward males.

So they struggle and question, rush and confront, retreat and hide, wonder and wander—these resilient saplings of our forest. I return to the image of the forest because it really seems to apply. They need cultivation, these young trees that appear to many adults as "wild" trees. Indeed, many of them are growing wildly, for lack of cultivation. Feeding, watering, pruning, watching—all the conscientious caring that is needed for the development of a powerful nation that can stand tall and withstand environmental abuse.

This book, then, is intended to help prevent that old saying, "Can't see the forest for the trees." It is meant to help you see our "trees"—our young ones as well as ourselves—for what we really have been, what we really are, and what we really can become. In doing so, I would be unforgivable if I tried to describe the entire "forest;" in fact, this is hopefully one small contribution. My efforts in this book are designed to emphasize the importance of opening our eyes when dealing with our young females, treating them honestly and with a conscious recognition of their significance for our future as a people. As another of my heroines, Mary McLeod Bethune, said in 1933, "The true worth of a race must be measured by the character of its womanhood."[1] We need to have our eyes on each tree as well as the forest as a whole.

Hopefully, this book is just one tool to help adults measure the character they are building within Black adolescent females. Like other books, this one provides a resource to which parents, teachers, counselors and other care-givers may refer to answer questions, clarify issues and get suggestions. I have tried to include helpful, hopeful and practical information about the development of Black adolescent females. But I have also remained mindful that it will always be parents who must be the primary character-builders and nurturers of children—even adolescents, with whom parents are frequently so much at odds. So Chapter Two, "The Home Front," is meant to examine the kind of relationships between Black parents and their adolescent daughters which occur during this most challenging stage of their offsprings' life.

In my desire to help those who want to help Black adolescent females, I have come to realize that part of my role is that of transmitter. If I am to help you "open your eyes" when it comes to perceiving Black adolescent females, one important way to do that is to present what they have to say about issues which concern them. So throughout this book there are anonymous comments, in their own words, about their relationships with family members, their friendships—with females and males—their neighborhoods, their free time and how they spend it, love and sex, parenting, being Black and being female. By relaying these comments, I hope to indicate the diversity of experiences among today's Black female young people; I also hope you will gain further clarity in your views of who they are and how they feel.

Yet this book would be incomplete if it concentrated solely on individuals; we live in a society which has yet to assign full peoplehood to African-Americans. Thus there is also an effort made to connect some of the forces—such as the continuing presentation of myths about Black people—which influence the quality of contact made with young Black females in the various situations they face from day to day. Chapter Three, "Her Friendships," continues the thread from the previous chapter by concentrating on two other kinds of relationships of great importance to young Black females: those they have with young Black males and those with their female peers.

With the aforementioned as a foundation, Chapter Four, "Approaching Change," addresses what has not worked in dealing with today's Black adolescent females and why a fundamental change in approach is necessary. This chapter targets the heart of the situation by focusing on the need for a *cultural* approach—the complete drawing closer of all that we as African-Americans believe and do, with the heart and soul of our future, our adolescent females. With this approach in mind, Chapter Five, "Nurturing Her Future: Practical Possibilities," introduces several examples of those from our past and present who enliven the Nguzo Saba, a set of starting points from which cultural character-building is possible.

As anyone working with young people knows, practical information is the best advice a book can provide, and this book would only partially succeed without a usable program. That is found in Chapter Six, "A Rites of Passage Program for You." The chapter outlines six areas to explore—sexuality, familyhood, community and friends, time/work/money, creativity, and being and becoming whole and proud. Hopefully, the program will provide a model for you to implement on a group basis.

There is a rites of passage program in this book for a definite reason. I firmly believe that one way we as a people can move successfully toward our collective future is by transplanting some of our successful traditions. One of those traditions is the use of a rite of passage which formalizes the development of our young into adulthood. Throughout the making of this book I have noticed the need for conscious and thoughtful cultivation of our adolescent females, and if this book helps in any way at all, I hope it is in the area of cultural cultivation. Chapter Six was written as a sincere attempt to contribute to cultural change; however, in applying the suggestions given, I would hope that participants revise the program according to their individual situations.

By now, you may have noticed that I do have a set of beliefs which embrace this book. Those beliefs include the following:

—Problems do exist in the development of today's Black adolescent females, and we should be aware of what the problems are and what/who causes them.

—Strengths also exist within and around today's Black adolescent females, strengths which are and should be reinforced and enhanced.

—Our adolescent females are a fundamental part of us as a culture and as individuals, and they must be cultivated and celebrated as the best of what we offer the world, today and for the future.

—Black adolescent females need a frame of reference that is culturally based and compatible with the best of our history.

—There is much that we can do to be their advocates, role models and teachers.

—If we believe that our adolescent females are the heart and soul of our future, we will do whatever we can, in the way we can, to encourage and reinforce positive self-images among them.

ACKNOWLEDGEMENTS

A great many people enabled me to write this book. There are too many to include here, so if I neglect to mention everyone's name, lack of space is the only reason. A few people, though, deserve particular praise and recognition.

First, I wish to express my appreciation to my publisher, Jawanza Kunjufu; his wife and colleague, Rita Kunjufu; and their staff at African American Images. They have continued to encourage me as I engaged in what became a complex process, and I am privileged to have had the opportunity to work with them.

Second, my gratitude is extended to Prof. Eloise Cornelius, School of Social Work, University of Illinois-Chicago, for her insightful contributions to my perspectives regarding Black female youth. She continued to be available whenever I requested her time and expertise. In addition, she has for many years been my "other mother" to whom I have looked for her example as a self-loving Black woman.

Third, Rev. Walter McCray, Black Light Fellowship, Chicago, has earned my deeply felt acknowledgment for his ongoing contributions of time, feedback, and equipment during the course of preparing this book for publication. He, too, is a model—of Black male leadership, scholarship and friendship.

My deep appreciation also goes to all the women and men whose work I was allowed to see in process as they focused their efforts on the productive development of young Black females. I thank all of you for your cooperation and your interest in my work.

The people whom I owe the greatest amount of praise are my family members. Throughout this time, they have demonstrated their faith in me with continued encouragement and patience. Thank you, one and all.

Lastly, it is God to whom all honor is due. My Maker made me write this book with the best of intentions, and I pray I have done my best effort.

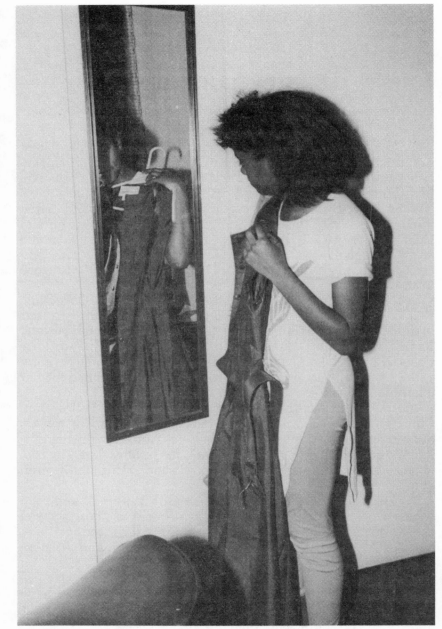

Throughout adolescence, she struggles to define herself.

HER MANY DEVELOPING SELVES

"I gave up some youth for knowledge, but my gain
was more valuable than my loss."

— Maya Angelou
I Know Why the Caged Bird Sings, 1970

Maya Angelou's words give us a significant clue to the
uniqueness of Black female adolescence. Trying to define that
stage of life, though, is both difficult and necessary. The task is
tough, because it might be tempting to simply attach the
dominant culture's theories of adolescence. But that would not
tell enough, for it would ignore the influence of culture. The job
is made more difficult when we recognize there is no single
definition; in fact, there are many forces at work which come
together to form stages of development and areas of growth.
Yet the job needs doing, because contributing to those stages
and areas becomes a frustrating, overwhelming responsibility
if one doesn't know what kind of development is in progress.

Who are these many developing selves, and what kind of
growth is underway? What is it about the development of a
Black female adolescent that is unique to Black females? How
would you define a female? I asked several young Black
females the latter question during a survey I conducted, and
these are some of their responses:[1]

"You have to act like a woman, be with women."
—a 12-year-old

"A very important part of human society."
—a 16-year-old

"The odd side of a male."

—a 15-year-old

"It means that I have to comb my hair every day, and I have to stay clean and do good in school."

—an 11-year-old

"A very intelligent person."

—a 15-year-old

"A tender feminine person."

—a 16-year-old

"The opposite of a male."

—a 14-year-old

"A lovely human being."

—a 15-year-old

"A female is very pretty; she can get pregnant."

—an 11-year-old

"A mature young lady that develops quick."

—a 15-year-old

Although these were not all the comments given, they represent both the range and the kind of responses as to what beliefs and behaviors define a female.

The Three Stages of Adolescence

For a long time, Americans viewed female adolescence in a simplistic manner. Whether their area of expertise made them mainly researchers or parents, most believed that this phase of life involved one chronological period of time—the teenage years—and for females, there was one event, menstruation, which hailed its beginning, and one event, marriage, which signalled its ending. At least for Caucasians, perhaps this vision of adolescence was once adequate. But for African-Americans, it has proven to be wholly inadequate.

It is necessary to look more closely at adolescence and to keep in mind that much of what was believed before will have to be relearned. By doing so, you enable your contact with adolescents to be more fully informed and sensitive to their reality.

Although there are no absolute boundaries between them, adolescence is marked by three stages:[2]

• early adolescence (also known as preadolescence), which usually begins between the ages of 10-14;

• mid-adolescence, which might take place between 14 and 17 years old;

• late adolescence, which might begin at age 17 and end at about age 20.

Within each of these stages there are particular areas of growth that form the foundation for progress to the next stage. Some adolescents make this movement to the next stage at earlier or later chronological ages than others. Therefore, the information that follows is meant to indicate signals of development, not to draw a rigid picture. Adolescence, you have probably noticed, refuses to welcome hard and fast rules about its definition.

However, it is possible to view each adolescent stage through some specific areas of growth: physical (which is identifiable mainly during early and mid-adolescence), intellectual, and social/emotional development. Within these areas of growth are some important clues to what an adolescent female is busily "working on" as she heads toward womanhood.

Early Adolescence

Physically speaking, several sex-related changes occur within girls at this point in their lives. Generally, they have their most rapid growth since their babyhood. Some obvious changes take place, such as growth in height, the first pubic hairs and budding of the breasts (in which the breasts begin to mound and the nipples begin to project outward). In addition, there are other changes which are definitely sex-related but not as visible: the size and structure of the reproductive system continue developing toward maturity. With the exception of the growth spurt, which usually continues throughout preadolescence, all these changes generally happen before menstruation. In short, the physical development of early adolescence is one of preparation.

At some point during female preadolescence, menstruation usually happens. Now the body, basically speaking, is "ready" for reproduction. In effect, menstruation marks the clear indication that a female is capable of conceiving another life. Every month thereafter, a female adolescent is reminded —often painfully reminded—that she can bear children. More than any other physical change, menstruation is the one event which shows a female that her body is working properly and she is growing up.

However, other growth is happening too. There are intellectual signals which can and do take place during preadolescence. (These signals are not sex-related; they are signals within the growth of males as well.) Her thinking is beginning to include less concrete information; she wonders, for instance, "what would happen if...," and "what is good and bad, and what makes something good and bad?" Although she is beginning to think more abstractly, during preadolescence, she is still working on it; therefore, she can't always make clear connections between decisions and their consequences. She is in the process of trying out her thinking on what interests her, so naturally she may show quite a lot of interest in various subjects. But she may quickly move from one subject to another within a period of time that—to adults—seems puzzling. To the preadolescent, it's just another part of her development.

It is perhaps in the area of social/emotional growth that preadolescence can strain adults' patience. That's because preadolescents, generally speaking, are beginning the biggest "move" since infancy—away from the simpler, more recognizable world of the family and toward the complex, often less familiar worlds of themselves, their peers, and their neighborhoods. In the area of social/emotional growth, there is no previous time during a child's life when so much is being dealt with for the first time.

Preadolescent females become focused on their physical changes; that's quite understandable, given what is taking place. Their preoccupation with themselves may result in them behaving in self-conscious ways (in which they might, for example, develop a slouched posture), or in hyper-conscious ways (in which they might seem to "flaunt" whatever part of their bodies is in their eyes developing well). Or they may shift from one kind of behavior to another, depending on how their peers act toward them or how family members react to their behavior. In addition, preadolescents may show other, more well-known indications of self-preoccupation, such as spending a greatly increased amount of time getting dressed, taking great care in fixing their hair, showing greater interest in cosmetics and other beauty products, etc. This self-absorbed behavior becomes frustrating to parents and other adult caregivers because it is inevitably combined with a period of lowered self-esteem. Frequently, preadolescents may make comments like: "I don't look right," "I'm not as pretty as...(whomever happens to be the most popular girl in her peer group, at least for the moment)," and there seems to be little if anything an adult can say or do to convince her otherwise. That's because of the other social and emotional changes which occur during this stage.

As she begins her move from the family circle, she must also begin to redefine family relationships. But this is only a beginning; often she still leans on family members for reassurance and guidance during this stage. As such, she may raise a few questions and push a little beyond the dependence she had before, but any major conflicts about her parents' authority are still ahead. What may seem very different to a parent or other older family member is that she is no longer quite as accepting of the relationship as she was at a younger age; she's more likely to express her view of, for instance, where she should go, with whom she ought to spend her free time, and when she's supposed to return home. What is important to point out here is that this is a trial period for the next stage of adolescence. The redefinition of her relationship with her family is in process; therefore, much of what happens between her and her parents and other relatives will have a very important effect on how family relationships go during mid-adolescence.

To many parents and other adult care-givers, it seems as though preadolescent females prefer their peers to their relatives. This is certainly true to a large extent, and for some important reasons. Peers become a key part of her life during preadolescence; something called the "herd instinct" begins to have a great influence over how she views herself. Because she often feels very uncertain about her physical changes, part of the reason she wants to be around her female peers is to reassure herself that there are others to whom the same or similar changes are happening. She can compare herself to them and decide whether her own changes are "normal" or "weird." Body changes aren't the only reason, though; she wants someone who is also experiencing the emotional changes—the interest in clothes, make-up, hairstyles; the worrying about beauty; and of course, the growing interest in the opposite sex.

During preadolescence, sexuality becomes an element of social and emotional growth. It is a frequent topic of discussion and a big reason for peer focus. As they develop physical changes that mark them as clearly different from males, and as their intellectual growth gives them the ability to wonder and judge more abstractly, preadolescent females get help from their female peers in defining themselves, sexually speaking, and to distinguish themselves from males. Peer assistance is also desired and obtained in terms of how to relate to the opposite sex.

Although much more will be said about peer relationships in Chapter Three, I think it's necessary to explain what I mean by "sexuality." Generally speaking, sexuality is being used in reference to the developing sense of femaleness, *not* the act of sexual intercourse and all that entails. It is critical to keep in mind that girls are attempting to draw a distinction between themselves and boys; at the same time, they're beginning to form that part of their identity which has to do with their gender. This kind of distinction seems necessary to make because the dominant culture has drawn such close connections to sexuality and sexual intercourse that at times there may seem to be no difference between the two—but there definitely is much more to sexuality than the act of sexual intercourse.

Mid-Adolescence
The physical growth which so rapidly occurred during early adolescence begins to slow down at this stage. The mid-adolescent female usually reaches the physical height she will remain for the rest of her life. Sex-related developments occur at this stage as well: her body fat increases around her hips, thighs, calves, and breasts; her pelvic region increases in diameter; and pubic hair growth increases. Although these developments are not required for reproduction—and hence it is known that preadolescents can conceive life—the mid-adolescent stage is usually when sex hormones activate the body changes which make a girl look "womanly." Physically speaking, it's during mid-adolescence when females usually take on the outward appearance of a woman.

Further intellectual preparation takes place during mid-adolescence that is built on what began at pre-adolescence. There is increased abstract thinking taking place, so concrete thinking begins to take more of a back seat. It becomes more possible for mid-adolescents to understand the consequences of decisions and actions; however, the intellectual "work" is still incomplete. Thus when it comes to the consequences of decisions, a mid-adolescent will not always use what she may understand. In addition, when a decision made or an action taken seems difficult or filled with emotion, she may not use the abstract thinking needed to recognize possible consequences or options; instead, she may retreat to the easier, concrete thinking about taking an action or making a decision.

Mid-adolescence brings with it some social and emotional growth as well. In terms of her view of herself, a mid-adolescent adjusts her former, lowered self-image; at least in terms of her physical self, she begins to feel more comfortable because she is achieving a body image which is more in line with that of a woman. But the view she has of herself is still under some self-questioning; as she closes the chronological gap between herself and adulthood, she wonders who she will be and what her life will be like. Of course, her increased ability to think in abstract terms reinforces and enhances this self-questioning.

During this stage, family relationships undergo their biggest conflicts. If a parent or other adult care-giver thought preadolescence had its problems, once mid-adolescence gets into full swing, they almost always point to this stage as the one most like a battlefield. There is major disagreement over who's in control, the teenager or the parent/care-giver; there may be so much conflict that communication breaks down to the point of lengthy periods of angry silence by both parties. As a mid-adolescent struggles for greater independence from her family and more control over her life, she may say and do things which are meant to make herself clearly separate from her parent/care-giver. Parental guidance and rules, at this stage, are often reminders to her that she is not separate and is not in control; in addition, some of what she says and does may be in definite opposition to what a parent believes. Thus, the conflict may increase and continue; in some cases, it may strain the family bonds to the breaking point.

As a mid-adolescent pushes herself away from family ties, she usually pushes herself more closely to her peers. The connections she began during early adolescence grow stronger and in her eyes, more necessary. However, she also begins to refine those ties and form close friendships with particular peers. In many cases, then, she doesn't wish to be around every peer she knows; she begins a more selective process of relating to peers. As her time away from home and family increases, so does her interest in chosen peers as ones with whom she wants to spend time doing what mutually interests them. These chosen peers become important as those to whom a mid-adolescent increasingly refers for help in making decisions that gain in complexity; in addition, chosen peers are increasingly depended upon for actions to take and day-to-day behavior that will, in turn, become a firmer part of her future. She is forming habits, then, which in her view have less to do with what a parent believes and more to do with her chosen peers' beliefs.

Of course, sexuality is also being addressed during mid-adolescence. As physical womanliness becomes more obvious, a mid-adolescent may move into acting on her belief in her femininity. In other words, she may increasingly test her ability to attract members of the opposite sex, and she may "experiment" on just what defines the borders of her sexual behavior. Basically, she is in the process of making up her own rules of sexual behavior. So of course, the nature of her family and peer relationships, as well as the kind of groundwork that has been laid during preadolescence, will have a great deal to do with what may happen in terms of a mid-adolescent's sexuality.

Late Adolescence

Physically speaking, most of what has happened during the previous stages is 95% of all that will take place in adolescence. A little more growth in height sometimes occurs, as does some additional increase in fat in the body areas mentioned during mid-adolescence. A few may show some physical development during late adolescence that usually occurs during mid-adolescence.

In terms of intellectual development, some important progress takes place. During late adolescence, there is the opportunity to gain mastery over complex thinking. Thus a late adolescent can not only understand consequences of decisions and actions, she can make better use of what she understands. It is increasingly possible, at this stage, for her to use and rely upon her intellectual powers to make a wide range of decisions about her life.

Although it may seem as though there isn't anything left which might develop, there are some emotional and social steps which can occur during late adolescence. Again, a late adolescent is building on what emerged in the two previous stages. Now that she is on the verge of adulthood, she feels an even stronger urge to completely define herself in specific, concrete ways. In addition, if her intellectual development has proceeded in even a generally progressive manner, she is capable of an enlarged view of a range of decisions to be made, such as: where she will live, how she will support herself, whether she will marry someone in the near future, and most of all, how she will get from where she is now to where she wants to (or thinks she ought to) be as a person of legal, adult age.

At this stage, family relationships may seem unimportant; in fact, there is sometimes little communication carried on between a late adolescent and a parent/care-giver. A truce of some sort has perhaps been worked out, but it might be a stalemate rather than a peaceful co-existence. To a late adolescent, a parent and the conflicts that happened during mid-adolescence may seem far in the past; on the other hand, the parent is rarely the one to whom a late adolescent goes for the kind of guidance or approval that was automatically sought during childhood.

Socially and emotionally, a late adolescent becomes more sophisticated. Her choice of friends may narrow—and she may end some friendships she used to enjoy as a pre- or mid-adolescent—or she may expand her circle of friends to include ones whom she believes are more in line with goals of a future that is much closer to her now. In addition, many of her habits and values are more definite to her, so her need for peers may be more in terms of reinforcing her values rather than helping her form them. Again, because she feels more specific and definite about her views and values, she usually believes she knows what she wants in terms of her sexuality. A late adolescent may not have achieved what she believes should be happening in the area of her sexuality, but she usually has some definite opinions about her femininity and her rules of sexual behavior.

Being and Becoming: Young Black Females

When it comes to describing Black female adolescence, it's quite a challenge trying to position them in stages. Adolescence is a complex period of life for any human. Society's myths regarding Black females tend to distort the ability to identify them truthfully, and the dominant culture's ambivalence toward young people means that, taken as a whole, it might appear impossible to shape any definite statements related specifically to Black female adolescents.

Nevertheless, I believe there are enough qualities of development, shared during certain stages of Black females' adolescence, to describe and thereby understand them more fully. Therefore, what has been outlined about the stages of adolescent development generally applies to Black females, but the information will be more understandable when examined in the context of the cultural identity being formed.

Throughout adolescence, Black females are struggling to define their cultural selves. This is basically a social, emotional and psychological struggle. Thus a Black female adolescent is seeking to understand what place her Blackness holds in her life, in her view of herself, how she feels about that view, and in what ways society influences her self-image. Questions which invariably must be addressed include: Who am I? Black? African-American? American? In addition, she struggles to decide the priorities of her self-image: Which is more important, the fact that I am Black or the fact that I am female? On top of those questions must come ones related to her struggle to personalize her cultural role: What part will I play in the present and future of my people?

Having introduced this journey of questioning, I do so knowing full well there may be many adults for whom these concerns seem entirely too sophisticated for youth. Impossible, the doubters respond. Black girls aren't mature enough; those questions don't occur to them until they're much older. Perhaps young Black females, particularly preadolescents, aren't stating the questions quite that way; yet they are often showing strong indications of an interest and a need to address these concerns.

Sexuality, "the quality or state of being either of two divisions distinguished respectively as male or female,"[3] is one of the "selves" that young Black females are trying to define. Forming a definition of their sexuality isn't easy, given the influencing confusion broadcast by forces such as those found in the media. Take, for instance, the images presented in these advertisements:

A company's new line of wearing apparel opens a commercial break on television. A girl of about fifteen is shown sprawled on her stomach across a bed, talking on the telephone. Next to her is a telephone book jammed with names and numbers. Her back is arched slightly, her lips are curved into a half-pout, and one of her hands caresses the pillow beside her. Overheard are these words: "What's between Jeri and her men? Just jeans." (Society's stereotyped "Jezebel," the sex object, is at work here: Jeri's packed phone book gives her lots of men to call; meanwhile, Jeri's "control" in the situation is clearly related to sexual intercourse, made evident by the fact that there's nothing between her and her men but a pair of pants, easily removed.)

A huge billboard ad, displayed across a well-traveled street in a Black community, shows a brown-skinned woman stretched out on a luxurious couch. A man with similar skin tone is leaning over her; his position makes him look like he's about to climb atop her. She's smiling seductively at him, and the caption reads: "All my men prefer me in musk...the fragrance that makes me irresistable!" ("Jezebel" is at it again. Not only is she so "powerful" that no man could possibly help but engage in sexual intercourse with her, she's unwilling to limit herself to just one man. Why should she? She's "irresistable.")

Confusion and contradiction—the stuff of which myths like "Jezebel" are made about Black womanhood—are paralleled in society's messages regarding youth. We live in a nation that can't make up its mind about the value or the role of young people. In the midst of society's indecision about its youth, Black female adolescents have still had to figure out personal definitions of their sexuality, even though several questions go unanswered: Are young people miniature adults—with the same needs, responsibilities, outlook on life, and inner view of themselves—or are they somehow different? If so, in what ways are they different? Are young people "good" or "bad"—isn't it to be expected that they're "bad"? Why can't we adults stay "young" forever—why can't we have what youths have?

As they try to steer their way through adolescence, young Black females are confronted with this society's unresolved view of youth. If an adult were to put herself in a Black adolescent female's shoes, the following messages are among those she would probably discover:

—advertisements (like the one featuring "Jeri") that portray "sexiness" at a preadult age; in fact, the ads make it clear that the model used is, legally speaking, nowhere near the age of consent for sexual intercourse;

—television talk shows on which so-called "beauty" products and cosmetic surgery are discussed with a great deal of excitement by the guests and audience alike; the products and operations involve body transformations designed to suck, pluck, pull and otherwise reject any sign of aging past the 21st birthday.

For a young Black female, the various messages tell her she's in a strange situation. If she believes the media

11

messages, she's supposed to be overwhelmed by her sex drive. Indeed, adult males are the ones she ought to go after, because her sex drive would supposedly require a "mature," "real" man's energy. So of course, she should dress and apply the make-up that would give her a grown-up—but not too grown-up because she might lose her appeal—appearance of sophistication and full knowledge of sexual intercourse. Is a preadult version of "Jezebel" calling her? She certainly is!

Clearly, the sexuality implied by media images of flashy or romanticized intercourse and reacted with secretive giggles and bug-eyed stares is not the whole truth. What, then, does female sexuality really mean?

Joyce Ladner's viewpoint comes to mind:

> The person she [a Black adolescent girl] is, the way she comes to feel and respond to events in her environment are highly conditioned by the cultural milieu. Thus, coming into womanhood in the Black community means that the environment largely shapes what kind of form and content her identity assumes.[4]

Ladner's suggestion, that young Black females are strongly influenced by what their cultures—both the American and the African-American—believe to be the standard of womanhood, is certainly reflected among the Black female adolescents I surveyed. "Be with women," "tender," "feminine," "stay clean," and "lovely" are definitely standards of belief and behavior which the dominant culture has long applied to the female sex. Coupled with those standards are ones more specifically related to the experiences of Black women. Because Black women have come to expect to handle a great deal of responsibility at a fairly young age, comments like: "Act like a woman," "A very important part of human society," "I have to...do good in school," and "A mature young lady that develops quick," indicate a continuation of this image.

Clearly, many of the comments connect femaleness with womanhood, and womanhood with certain jobs to tackle. In other words, there seems to be the attitude that adolescence has brought many of these young Black females closer to adulthood, and they know they will be depended upon to take an important role. If we agree that environmental forces have been a significant influence in molding this kind of attitude, the image of the hardworking, responsible Black woman has certainly gone a long way toward combating stereotyped images like "Jezebel."

Of course, there were also comments which related a female to a lovely, tender, feminine person. In addition to being statements that mirror the dominant culture's image of femaleness, there is another force at work here. Interestingly, the words "person" and "human being" were included when words like "feminine" and "tender" were used. The matching of these terms suggests a sophisticated understanding of themselves as beyond a limited view of only being gender-related but also people-related. In short, if a Black adolescent female defines her gender as tied, even partially, to the human family, she has taken some significant steps toward a broader, more mature view of her sexuality.

It has already become a well-established truth that, when it comes to Black female adolescents, they are quite mature in many areas of their development. Joyce Ladner was one of the sociologists to point this out. In her groundbreaking book, *Tomorrow's Tomorrow*, Ladner states:

> These girls are influenced by a set of traditions, a common value system and a set of beliefs that, although varying from group to group, are still shared to some extent by all of them. Their aspirations for being the hard-working backbone of the family, for children, for an education and for a kind of spiritual empathy—the ability to understand and develop the necessary resources to fight oppression and make healthy adaptations to what are sometimes overwhelming circumstances—are common features.[5]

Thus, if we examine Black female adolescents with the kind of perspective that Ladner suggests, we can address the various stages of development and areas of growth in a unique manner. In doing so, questions like "Who am I?" and "Which is more important, my Blackness or my femaleness?" become inevitable; they cannot be dismissed as "too sophisticated," because they are in fact the basic questions to ask. In short, young Black females are aware they don't exist in a vacuum; they are part and parcel not only of human development, but of institutional racism and sexism as well.

So the issue that would probably be best discussed at this point would be the idea that young Black females are, generally speaking, more mature than their Caucasian female peers. Anyone who has regular contact with Black female adolescents may feel a tendency to agree with this idea. After all, it has been asserted that young Black females mature physically at a fairly young age (in part because they have been fed a diet that includes a great proportion of red meat[6]). Perhaps they even seem to proceed through their physical development at a faster rate, so the age ranges I have given for adolescent stages may seem to need some narrowing. In addition, young Black females may seem further advanced at younger ages in certain aspects of their social and emotional growth. They may indicate this growth in terms of their behavior toward males, their styles of dress, and the relative speed with which they come to terms with what they must do in order to take on adult roles. In other words, rather than spending years being self-absorbed with questions of "Who am I?" they move quickly past that to ask, "What do I need to do to become a woman?" Mary Burgher examined several autobiographies of Black women and found, among other things, a common thread of early maturity among them. In part, Burgher related this maturity to the society they faced:

> The Black woman's need to grow up fast, by-passing a leisurely childhood, emanates from harsh environmental conditions coupled with strong interdependent and intraresponsible familial relationships. The collective consciousness inherent in "We're all in this together" and "We must do it for ourselves or do without" necessitates adult awareness, grown-up strength, and independence at a very early age. Thus, more often than not, the route to Black womanhood is fast and direct.[7]

In other words, Burgher and Ladner make it clear that in spite of racism and sexism, young Black females have demonstrated an ongoing capacity to cope with difficult circumstances and overcome them. This is, in effect, their pool of resourcefulness that has been our cultural wealth for centuries. A question like, "What do I need to do to become a woman?" occurs to a Black adolescent female because she has a unique ability to understand that she *must* ask; her very survival depends on it.

You may recall that this is the kind of question which, intellectually speaking, belongs to the stage of late adolescence. Indeed, it represents a level of abstract thinking that is quite mature. In addition, there are other indications—in areas such as employment, familyhood, spirituality, and a Black female adolescent's attitudes toward her neighborhood—that show definite signs of developing maturity. There is a great deal of

14

good news to share about young Black females, and in the next two chapters I will give you several examples of the wealth of information to be discovered about them, in their own words.

However, this chapter would be incomplete if I left you with the impression that all is fine with their development. In fact, there are some disturbing patterns that cannot go ignored. Earlier I suggested that perhaps some adults refuse to believe there are so many stages of development and areas of growth among Black female adolescents. There seems to be a growing viewpoint among adults that somehow, since young Black females seem so mature and capable of handling life's often tough circumstances, we should therefore look the other way when it comes to elements of social, emotional, and intellectual development. They'll be all right, this viewpoint argues, they don't really need much help. Besides, if we apply too much attention to this kind of development, Black adolescent females may become too focused on self-identity; perhaps they'll even get selfish to the point of ignoring the needs of the rest of Black people.

But if we examine Black female adolescents and assume they do need physical, social, emotional, and intellectual development to become whole and complete adults, we must challenge ourselves to address some concerns in ways that are unique to this group of people. For example, in a situation in which a 15-year-old Black female has just learned she is pregnant, are we to conclude that she has developed the emotional, social, and intellectual tools she will need to adequately deal with that new aspect of her life? Or, in another situation, in which a 16-year-old Black female is experiencing so much trouble at home that she believes she has no other choice but to leave, how will we be able to tell whether she is armed with the emotional, intellectual, and social maturity to have chosen the wisest course? My point here is not to attempt any instant, simple guesswork; instead, I caution us as adults involved with young Black females that we must be ever careful in our judgments about a very complicated group of people.

More simply stated, Black adolescent females defy simplification. One of them may have the physical appearance and chronological age of a 19-year-old, the emotional development of a 14-year-old, and the intellectual capacity of an 18-year-old. Another one may be 10 years old, physically appear to be around 16 years old, and demonstrate the intellectual development of an 8-year-old and the emotional capacity of a 17-year-old. Very rarely do any young Black females proceed through adolescence as though it's a route marked by neat, easily identified phases. Society does not allow that kind of journey for them, and circumstances hardly ever present themselves so predictably.

Far from desiring that kind of journey for them (it's beyond my or any other adult's power to provide and control it to that extent), I believe the time has long since come when we *must* include greater emphasis on social, emotional, and intellectual development during the adolescent period of a Black female's life. African-Americans have unique experiences to bring to these areas of growth; what is needed is a more conscious effort given to how our culture can contribute to these areas within our female adolescents. This is particularly relevant if we are to help them shape their futures beyond the present existences in which most of them live. Simply said, any parent desires that her child have a better life than the parent experienced. If that is to happen, we can no longer hope or expect that the dominant culture will take the major steps to make that a reality; this kind of viewpoint allows far too many of our young people to fall victim to the same oppression we and our forebears faced. A better life, then, will require that more tools be used; certainly those tools include what can be developed socially, emotionally, and intellectually.

Given where they live, and the conditions of racism and sexism under which they live, young Black females are giving up some youth for a certain kind of knowledge. By looking at them fully—in all their stages and areas of development—we have taken an important step toward helping them gain more than what society has forced them to lose. Now we need to look at the most basic level at which they develop all these selves—the home front.

THE HOME FRONT

PRY....

why do people pry? why can't I make my own decisions?
so many voices telling me what to do who to see
who not to see,
must be the right kind of boy from the right family—
"what do his mother and father do?"
   "where do they live?"
   "where does he go to school?"
   "where does he go to church?"
all those questions make me feel like I should
meet boys armed with a survey sheet—
"please check off all applicable answers"
   feel like a ginger ale bottle
   when the lid comes off,
   release let steam go offfffff—want to scream—ssssshh,
reasonable questions they just want to know
   it's concern, they care
   is it really caring
   what's the difference between caring and prying?
   will answering those questions guarantee care/love?
   is there a guarantee, a quick easy road to love?
   don't know don't know, feel cornered feel angry
   angry before, angry again, cornered again
   back at the beginning, when will this end
   don't believe growing up will automatically bring me easy
answers
      (when I reach 21 will I have
      an invisible survey sheet
      to help me know
      "right" men vs. "wrong" men?)
what's the missing ingredient—do I have to make mistakes to
understand?

confusing, thoughts tangled
wish parents would give me better clues
instead of long lectures and endless questions—already have
plenty of questions,
no answers.[1]

One day, during one of my occasional "sweeps" in which I try to make room for the mountain of files I've created with my writing, I found this poem. As I read it, a wave of memories surrounded me. I had written the poem during my adolescent years; I can't remember exactly when, or what "crisis" had prompted the words. However, I can remember how I felt—a rush of emotions swirled within me and it seemed at the time as though I was under the power of those feelings. Perhaps in reading "PRY" you will begin to sense the mixed emotions that so often embrace the day-to-day world of Black female adolescents. "PRY," then, provides a hint of the reactions many of them have to their relationships with their parents. The discussion of "the home front" begins with Black mothers and daughters.

Black Mothers and Daughters

The relationship between an African-American mother and her adolescent daughter carries with it a challenge: from the mother's point of view, she feels a responsibility to encourage great maturity at a relatively fast rate; thus the saying, "raising daughters but loving sons" is at the core of her attention. Meanwhile, her adolescent woman-child may receive this challenge with mixed emotions; on the one hand, she may certainly desire independence from the confines of her home and the control her parents have over her life, but she may also be aware of the tough struggle required of living on her own. In addition, she may understandably resent the different treatment and attitude her mother shows toward her versus any male siblings she may have. Why should I be the one to carry out domestic responsibilities, she may demand to know; why is the load on me if women are supposed to be equal to men? In spite of any resentment she may feel, she may need her mother's advice and support regarding some tough, survival-based issues such as employment, job or pay discrimination, child care, gang crimes, and rape. What is the status of today's Black mother-daughter relationship? I will begin to answer that question first by presenting some situations in which Black mothers

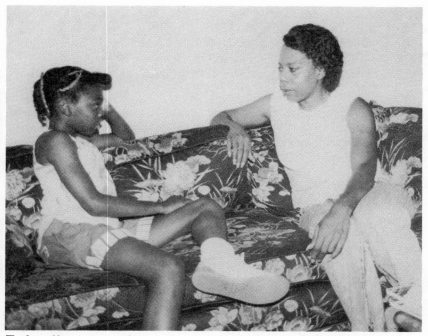

To be effective, mothers must communicate with their daughters.

and their daughters deal with their day-to-day relationship.

It has been in the arena of the home that Black mothers have focused to shape an alternative force within their daughters. In this environment a Black mother can actively fight racism and sexism; she can show she is a good woman by being an understanding one; she can demonstrate her toughness by exercising discipline about housework and homework; and she can relax enough to be an example of how a good-natured attitude can refresh what may otherwise be gloomy conditions. In the space of her home, a Black mother has often been an effective activist.

Other avenues continue to present opportunities for a Black woman to model the role of an activist. One of them is at her daughters' school:

First Impressions

I first met "Mrs. James" and her three daughters during a visit I made to their school. It is definitely *their* school; "Delia" is a second grader there, while her twin sisters "Shana" and "Sharice" are in seventh grade. "Mrs. James" works in the school office. She is a volunteer who comes every school day, and she concentrates mainly on record-keeping. Budget cuts have eliminated the position as a paid one, so her presence is obviously critical to the school's operation.

When I walked into the office to get directions to a classroom, "Mrs. James" asked, "What's the matter? You incognito today?"

I was startled at first; then I realized I had neglected to remove my prescription sunglasses when I came inside the building. "Beg your pardon, ma'am," I found myself saying to a woman who looked about the same age as I am. Needless to say, I now remind myself to take my sunglasses off as soon as I enter a building. "Mrs. James" is still with me.

By making sure she contributes as much as she can to the successful running of her children's school, "Mrs. James" enlarges her role of motherhood to embrace activism outside her home. It might have seemed rude or abrupt for her to speak to me the way she did, but I felt only gratitude—the same kind of response, in fact, I probably would have had if it had been *my* mother who said it. That old saying, "only a mother's love" is what I believe motivates Black women like "Mrs. James." In such a Black mother's love is the alertness to details like another Black female who wears sunglasses in a place such as a school, where Black children meet some people who have a tremendous effect on their development.

I believe there are quite a few "Mrs. Jameses" in Black communities across this nation, who do everything they can to spread their impact on their children's growth beyond their homes. I am also aware that, try as they do, situations do arise in which it may appear to outside observers that they have done little if nothing. Something like that happened to "Toni Washington" and her daughter "Ella":

An Unexpected Visit

"Hi Mrs. Washington, what's the trouble? You look so worried." The nurse at the neighborhood clinic sat next to a stoop-shouldered Black woman who was wiping her eyes.

"Hi Mrs. Jackson. I'm here with my Ella—she's in there," Mrs. Washington said, pointing to a nearby examining room. "I swear I believe I'm at the end of my rope. You know, me and Ella been comin' here for four years now, but I never thought we'd be here for something like this. Ella's pregnant. Doctor's in there talking with her about it now."

Nurse Jackson nodded and sat back. She guessed Mrs. Washington would talk if she wanted her to listen.

Toni Washington shook her head, as though to clear her thoughts. "I just can't figure it out. That girl had everything goin' for her—you know, she graduates next week."

The nurse smiled. "That's right! I remember you telling me when you were here a few months ago. Both of you were so excited..."

"That's just it—*both* of us were excited about her goin' to college. I always felt like we were making this effort together, with her studying and me singing her praises all the way. And now this. You know how she says it happened? She swears she never had sex with nobody until she went on a trip sponsored by the youth group at church. A church boy did it! I don't so much care if he went to church as much as I can't understand how this could have happened to my Ella—as hard as we both worked. Feels like now she'll have to start all over again, and nothin' will ever be the same."

Like "Mrs. James," "Mrs. Washington" may be a pseudonym but she's based on a real person.[2] A relationship like the one she has with her daughter is undergoing severe tests that would exhaust any mother's capacity to conduct and sustain her role as a facilitator of her daughter's progress. Teenage pregnancy is not restricted to Black females from low-income families. Events like pregnancy happen to young females from a variety of backgrounds and with diverse aspirations for their future. Varied as they might be, one of the consequences of adolescent pregnancy is a motherhood that is much more likely to encounter a poverty level of existence. And when that happens, a great deal more tends to occur as well, as "Tina Bertrand" can tell you:

Trouble Everywhere I Look

I know I'm gettin' close to the end of my rope. Can't deal with all this much longer 'cause it's been happenin' to me for too long. Been tryin' to get off welfare for 15 years, ever since my baby Maya was born. I don't want no welfare, I want a job. But I dropped out of high school when I had Maya and never went back. Only jobs seem to come my way don't pay nothin' —why a person could barely get there and back on that kind of money! Every other day seems like somebody's callin' up here to tell me my son's in trouble: the school, the police, you name it, that boy's done everything this side of bein' in prison. And Maya, she went and had herself a baby three years ago so now I'm babysittin' 'cause I told her she better go on and get her G.E.D. before life passes her right on by. That's what it's done to me, just passed me by.

"Tina Bertrand" feels a sense of hopelessness that has seeped into her life and is overwhelming her. Rather than passing her by, life has filled her space with so many hurdles that feeling inadequate to deal with them is a natural response. If one or two of the difficulties she faces appeared in her life, "Tina Bertrand" might certainly believe she could overcome them. But she is confronted with a son who has become a delinquent, a daughter who has followed in her footsteps and now has a child of her own, and meanwhile "Ms. Bertrand" lacks a high school diploma and job skills that might give her a chance to achieve a better income level. To an outsider, she might seem to be a failure; the greater concern, though, is that she believes she has failed in her life, that it is over and that her daughter is at risk of encountering the same kind of restrictions.

The subject of pregnancy usually brings to mind sexual intercourse. How does a Black mother deal with the issue of her daughter's initiation to this event? "Karen Hill-Blanchard" and her daughter "Shawn" experienced it this way:

Time for a Talk

"Mom, we have to talk," Shawn said as she sat next to her mother on the couch.

"Okay honey," her mother replied. She sensed something in her daughter's voice that seemed like they were about to get into quite a conversation.

"Mom, I've been thinking about something that I want to tell you about." Shawn took a deep breath and paused. Would her mother be as understanding about this as she usually was with everything else, she wondered. Well, I won't find out until I say what's on my mind, Shawn thought. "I've decided I'm ready to have sex with Ron. I want to go get a diaphragm and it'd be nice if you went with me." There. She'd said what she had been turning over in her mind for several weeks.

"Nice? What...what about...you..." The words tumbled from Mrs. Hill-Blanchard's mouth as though she'd lost control. A wave of thoughts hit her so hard, she became speechless. What am I to say to my daughter, she wondered. If I object, she'll probably go get one and have sex anyway. If I say okay, will it seem like I approve? What if she gets pregnant—there's no guarantee that she won't, especially if she uses a diaphragm. How can I feel sure she won't think that because she's started having sex with Ron, she's in love with him, and what if her future plans begin to seem less important than being in love? How can I help her postpone what I really feel is a mistake for this time in her life? Shawn, you're so young, she said silently, what's your hurry to grow up?

This is just the kind of scene that mothers dread. It forces them to confront their role versus that of their daughter's emerging journey away from home and family. A situation like this one brings with it issues of communication, female sexuality, males, and the future—all wrapped around a time period when mothers and daughters may either tiptoe around each other, trying to maintain harmony, or else they never seem to stop battling with each other over trivial matters that are unrelated to the real issues at hand.

How "Shawn" and her mother handle "Shawn's" announcement depends quite a bit on "Mrs. Hill-Blanchard's" attitudes toward intercourse in general and her feelings about her own experiences with sexual intercourse. Another factor will be whether she has laid some groundwork for this situation by making clear her attitudes through her behavior and her conversations with her daughter. So in this scenario, the fact that "Shawn" has approached her mother and initiated a discussion about intercourse indicates that she feels comfortable communicating with her mother about a sensitive, personal matter. In addition, her intention to get a diaphragm tells her mother that she wants to postpone pregnancy. Even though "Shawn" hasn't mentioned why she prefers not to conceive a child right now, she may have many reasons and her mother is probably aware of them. Thus, openings exist in the situation that present opportunities for the two females that should be treated as avenues for further communication.

Communication, then, is one of several important ingredients in an effective mother-daughter relationship between Black females. When it comes to communication, a Black mother might ask herself questions like these:

1. In what ways am I using the sending and receiving of messages to act out my roles of model and facilitator? (Is communication with my daughter a one-way arrangement or are

various opportunities used to encourage receiving messages as well as sending them?)

2. Do I see the possibility of learning something from my daughter, and is that as valuable to me as what I want to teach her?

3. Does my daughter get the impression through my communication that I know everything and have all the answers? Do I act like nothing phases me, troubles me, perplexes me?

4. On the other hand, do I give my daughter the impression through my communication that I fail to find answers, that life troubles me and confuses me?

5. Are there any subjects—such as intercourse, masturbation, and homosexuality—that I have placed off limits in our communication? Or can my daughter introduce any subject with me?

At this time in a daughter's life, friendships tend to pull her away from her relationship with her mother. As they do, the following questions might enable mothers and daughters to sustain their relationship:

1. In what ways am I handling this part of my daughter's life? Do I acknowledge the value she increasingly places on her friends, or am I saying and doing things that give her the impression I don't recognize the importance friends have for her?

2. Do I strongly oppose her choice of friends and if so, what are my reasons (for instance, are her friends' habits and preferences seen by me as counterproductive or negative because they don't care about school, they're gang members, or they have a reputation for using drugs)? Or are my reasons related less to bad habits and more to personal biases that may be unfounded (for example, are some of her friends teenage mothers and I'm afraid that my daughter will get pregnant if she hangs around them)?

3. Do I take seriously the modeling of friendships? Do I keep in mind that the kind of friends I have will affect the way my daughter views her own friendships?

4. Does the role my friends play in my life imply that, as an adult, friendship is a valuable part of my life or an insignificant part?

The opposite sex is also important to a young Black female and as such, males contribute to the quality of her relationship with her mother. The following questions may serve as a set of guidelines to evaluate the role that young males play in a mother-daughter relationship:

1. When it comes to males, in what ways do my daughter and I deal with them? By my statements and actions, do I transmit a message that Black adult males are a problem or a non-problem in my own life?

2. What do I have to say about the Black males who are my daughter's peers? Is my overall message that she should distrust, baby, encourage, or befriend them? Am I sending any mixed messages about her male peers?

3. What about my daughter's father? What do I have to say about him and how do I generally treat him?

4. Have I made my daughter aware of the historical image of Black men and society's racist treatment of them?

5. Do I count any males as among my friends, or are the males I know counted only as lovers or economic providers?

6. Are there any family members—father, grandfathers, brothers, uncles, cousins, and the like—whose close contact and familiarity with my daughter might contribute to her developing a positive *and* realistic view of Black males?

How a Black female adolescent spends her time can be a significant clue to the kind of mother-daughter relationship she has, because it reflects ways in which mother and daughter make priorities, take care of responsibilities and explore interests. These questions may help you focus on time in your relationship with your daughter:

1. What are my opinions about how my daughter should spend her waking hours? How do I communicate those opinions—by a communicative approach that accounts for receiving her views, by example, by force, by a combination of all these methods?

2. How do I deal with the process of making priorities when it comes to time? Am I too easy on her or too hard on her time use?

3. Is my daughter using some of her time to take care of domestic responsibilities like cooking, cleaning and laundry?

4. As I look ahead, what do I think will be the effect of the ways my daughter now spends her time on her adult years? How do I show her how I feel about that effect?

Questions such as these about friends, time, communication and males, are raised to help mothers lay some important groundwork. The subjects represent some of the most common, abiding topics that mothers and daughters deal with. Traditionally, African-American mothers transmit as much knowledge as they can to their daughters, as an effective way to prepare them for womanhood. However, fathers should not be overlooked and their importance is the emphasis of the next section.

Our Fathers and Their Daughters

In his article, "Africanity," Wade Nobles points out that "the critical issue is not the household *makeup* but the household *process*."[3] His perspective lends a refreshing angle of view toward African-American families and keeps us from getting distracted by arguments about the supposed "Black matriarch." As Nobles explains:

> What is important to understand, in this society particularly, is that what has been critical in black families is not whether it's female-headed or male-headed, but whether the *survival of the tribe* (family) was maintained.[4]

So Black fathers—even when they play little or no structural role in their daughters' everyday lives—have a process role to play that will aid the survival and quality of Black family life and the adolescent development of their daughters.

What does that process involve? When a father's role is pro-

Black fathers have special gifts to give to their daughters.

cess-oriented, he contributes to the development of attitudes and values concerning his daughter's selection of a mate with whom she intends to spend her adult life, as well as the males with whom she just means to have an evening out. Her father, by example and discussion, also gives her some initial clues as to what Black men are like. His function includes one of informing her about the historical effects of the conditions under which he now lives, for if he doesn't give her that information, she may enter adolescence and then adulthood with a misunderstood impression of the Black males in her culture. Day-to-day preparation is part of his role too; she will be greatly helped if he uses his role to warn her about some of the dangers, so she might sidestep as many of them as she can. Finally, his preparation should embrace whatever opportunities he can make available to her so he can encourage her to use them to their fullest. When a father's role is process-oriented, he contributes significantly to the way in which his children grow and understand themselves and their environment.

At this point, it might be useful to get a glimpse at some actual ways in which Black fathers today are demonstrating their role with their daughters. One of them is "Jeremiah Dobson" and his daughter "Pat":

Promises Made and Kept

The time for high school graduation had come. As Pat waited her turn to get her diploma, she looked over the audience. Smiling, she noticed her father sitting near the front. As she waved to him, she thought about their last conversation.

It was two weeks before her senior prom, and her father had told her he would not be able to buy her a graduation gift. He'd looked so sad when he said, "Pat, I really thought that bonus check would come through. But my company's going through some tough times so they cut back. If only I'd taken that night job . . ."

She'd interrupted him by giving him a big hug. "Daddy, I know you're trying. Why I wouldn't have had a prom dress if it wasn't for you. Don't you worry, I don't mind. Just seeing you there will be all I want."

And here he was, just like he promised. He had a way of doing that—keeping his promises as much as he could. When the ceremony was over, she rushed over to his side. Maybe it was the excitement of the day, or the memory of their last conversation. Suddenly a wave of memories washed over her, and she pictured all the good times she'd spent with her father. Big tears rolled their way down her cheeks, and when she wiped her eyes she realized he was crying too.

This scene highlights what Wade Nobles has called "the hidden strength in black families" because within this force is the capacity to push beyond the barriers of America's individualistic, technological drive—which so often motivates family members away from each other. Instead, forces like the ones displayed by "Pat" and her father embrace a kinship that is interdependent and personalized. In this kind of kinship, a Black father and his daughter can support and encourage each other, regardless of economic difficulties or disappointments. Nobles explains:

> The family is, therefore, experienced not only on a quasi-biological level by all its members, but it is also experienced as a veritable institution of *social solidarity* and *psychological security*.[5]

The security needed by a developing Black woman can be provided in a variety of ways and situations. "Darnell Thomas" was asked to give that kind of security by his daughter "Denice" and it emerged in what was for him an unexpected situation:

Not for Men Only

One evening, Darnell Thomas' telephone rang. His daughter Denice was on the other end.

"Hi Daddy," she said. "I want to talk to you 'cause I need your advice. I've been thinkin' about joining one of the teams at my school. But I can't decide whether to be on the basketball or the track team, and I can't be on both of them. What do you think?"

Her father didn't answer at first. The basketball or track team? he asked himself. What's she doin' with herself these days? "I don't know, honey," he replied. "What's the point of bein' in sports? That's for men, not for you. You need to concentrate on keepin' yourself pretty and feminine, so you'll get yourself a good husband."

Denice didn't respond. I can't understand why he can't see things my way, she thought. It's not like I just got interested in sports; I've been runnin' fast as far back as I can remember, and I like basketball. I'm pretty good at it too.

"But Daddy, the coaches at my school tell me if I keep up my sports I might get a college scholarship. They've noticed I'm good."

Her father's voice became angry as he said, "Look, I don't care what those coaches been tellin' you, you listen to me. What do they know? Girls don't get college scholarships for sports, they get 'em 'cause they're smart. You want to be smart, you'll pay attention to your daddy." With that, he hung up the phone.

Obviously, "Darnell Thomas" is against girls in sports. In fact, he's so biased about it, he has chosen not to keep himself informed about the growing involvement of young females in the sports arena. This involvement has been partly due to the progress made by implementing Title IX of the 1972 Equal Education Amendment Act passed by Congress. It has been reinforced wherever school sports departments have taken steps to include female students in their programs. However, "Mr. Thomas'" attitude is not that unusual. As Ernestine Mason, a high school athletic director, noted:

> Comments from peers and even adults abound that she can throw a ball and run "like a boy".... The myth that "girls are not really interested in sport but in boys" is supported by the low rate of participation of girls as compared to boys in sport. The low participation rate, however, is more likely a reflection of lack of opportunity and fear of being thought masculine than a lack of interest.[6]

Sports has always been viewed as the arena for males, mainly because of its association with strength and virility. Female athletes, then, have always been seen as "freaks" or "tomboys" and even though we can point proudly to some outstanding Black female athletes, they are still relatively few in number and they tend to be concentrated in just a few sports. Dr. Larry Hawkins, head of the Office of Special Programs at the University of Chicago, observes that he still has difficulty convincing Black mothers to let their daughters pursue their interest in sports. Yet he continues to try because, as he says, sports is "where a girl can feel a sense of worth without giving up her body to do it."[7]

So "Mr. Thomas" may not realize it but his daughter's interest in sports can be a healthy, productive avenue for her growth. Through sports involvement, she can develop a more positive self-image, and if she continues her involvement she can gain entrance to college on an athletic scholarship. If he will reconsider his personal opinions and encourage her, he may even give his relationship with her an opportunity to grow. "John Jones" saw an opportunity for him to initiate an awareness within his daughter "Johnnie" that he believed would help her:

An Ounce of Prevention

Mr. Jones had decided it was time to warn his daughter. He sat her down at the kitchen table one Saturday morning. "We need to talk about something important, Johnnie," he told her. "Now, don't frown at me 'cause this is not about something you did. I don't want you to think I'm just here to lecture you."

Johnnie smiled slightly. I wonder what he's getting at? she thought. He seems serious.

"I think it's time I said a few things to you, to warn you about something. You know what rape means?" he asked.

She nodded. "Think so."

"Well, maybe you do and maybe I need to make sure you do. You're 11 years old now, and it seems like every time I turn around, you're gettin' older. With me not being around you all the time, I get to thinking about you and I do worry sometimes. Your mother and I have always tried to make things clear to you so you'll understand. Rape is one of the things you need to be clear about 'cause it won't be too long before you start going out on dates. Between now and then, I want to make sure you know just what rape is."

"But what's rape got to do with dates?" Johnnie asked. Now she felt confused. She thought she knew about rape, but she didn't feel too sure about it now.

"Well, most dates haven't got anything to do with rape, as long as the girl makes as sure as she can that she's in control of the situation. And on a date, unless you know what you're doin', you may be so busy havin' a good time, that you forget to see the warning signs."

"Like what?" his daughter asked.

"Oh, there's usually some signals being sent. For instance, if he acts like all of a sudden he can't remember the route to drive you home, and he gets to drivin' a different way—that's a definite sign that something's not right. Or if you're with a group of kids at first, and he makes some excuse about havin' to separate you from the group, that's another sign. See, if you're not watching out, you may fool yourself into thinking that he just wants to be alone with you so he can get romantic. But unless you've both talked about it beforehand and you've agreed that's what you want to do, stuff like that can lead to rape."

Johnnie nodded silently. This was something to think about. "What else? Tell me some more, Daddy," she requested.

"Why don't we go over to the community center?" he suggested. "There's a meeting today about rape prevention, and I think if we both go, we'll be able to talk more about it."

"Okay," his daughter said. "That's a good idea."

Once again, some "hidden strengths" make themselves known between a Black father and daughter. "Mr. Jones" shows us that he feels confident enough about his role to be able to initiate a discussion of a subject that his daughter will find very useful as she spends more time around males and meets more males she wants to get acquainted with. Since she's still fairly young, she probably still feels the need for support and advice from her father, so this is an excellent time to talk about something like rape. In addition, her father's comfort level with her indicates his ongoing involvement; he is maintaining his interest in a relationship with "Johnnie."

By positioning his conversation around a subject he knows she's interested in (dating), "Mr. Jones" paves the way for introducing the seriousness of rape. More importantly, his approach gets her to view rape as a possible part of everyday life —in that way, she will be better prepared for it if it happens. And by attending a rape prevention meeting *together*, father and daughter have further opportunities to review and discuss as time goes on. This is a way to promote communication, and whatever happens to "Johnnie," it's likely that her father will be there to encourage her.

Situations like these three indicate just a few of the diverse interactions many Black fathers have with their adolescent daughters. In fact, all three "stories" are based on actual father-daughter relationships it has been my privilege to discover. The scenarios were chosen to highlight the process role that is manageable, regardless of a father's presence in his daughter's home or her mother's life. All the scholarly disagreement about the effects of a Black father's absence from his children's home life will probably continue as long as there are divorces and separations. To review this literature now may cloud the issue and return us to the days of what I call the "Moynihan reactions."[8] What is perhaps more helpful here is to emphasize to Black mothers and fathers alike the following points:

• If it is possible, if a daughter's father is willing to try, and if it is productive—if he has not shown pathological tendencies or behavior that suggests to a mother that he will not be a positive contributor to a daughter's development—he should be continually encouraged to get involved and stay involved in his daughter's life.

• Black fathers can embark on a special relationship with their daughters, one which enhances a mother's role. Whether they have money, a college degree, or an expensive car is not the issue; what is so much more important is whether they want to help their daughter in terms of emotional support and psychological encouragement.

Beyond the less tangible ways of being a provider, Black fathers can help provide the benefits of enculturation. With an eye toward us as a people, Black fathers can go a long way toward introducing a family-oriented, survival-based perspective that is uniquely African-American.

Day-to-Day Issues

In their everyday lives, young Black females and their parents encounter several issues which affect and are influenced by the kind of relationships they have with their mothers and fathers. How do Black adolescent females and their parents deal with situations involving clothes, music, cosmetics, domestic responsibilities, drugs and alcohol, school, and religion? Are these and other issues what cause the arguments that mark so much of adolescence? Do any Black families with adolescent offspring manage to avoid fighting about these concerns? When confronted with issues like drugs and clothes, how do Black mothers and fathers manage to convince their adolescent daughters to maintain the values they've tried to implant? Take a look at the examples provided in the situations that follow.

Burning up the wires

Tina, age 14

Mama says I'm boy crazy, got it bad. She's always naggin' at me to slow down. But I never really paid much attention to her or Daddy until the day after Jerald's mother called.

I've been hot on Jerald's trail for a couple of weeks. My friend Anita told me he liked me—she said she knew it was true 'cause she caught him staring at me twice in homeroom. So I figured the best thing to do was go for it.

First I asked him for his phone number. I couldn't tell for sure if he really liked me, all he did was shrug and ask me what for. I told him, "What you mean, 'what for'? Why does anybody ask for a phone number—so I can call you!" He smiled a little, then he gave me his number.

Well, that was pretty much what I needed—just a smile and a number, and I got to work on him. I've been callin' Jerald ever since, as many times as I can get to the phone. A lot of times, I don't get to talk to Jerald when I call. His mama answers the phone, which is not really what I like to have happen. She just as soon not let me talk to Jerald, at least that's the way it seems to me. I can't tell if she's lyin' or not when she says, "He's not here," or "He can't come to the phone right now." The other day she got mad at me and told me, "Look, girl, it's entirely too late to be callin' here. Don't you know what time it is? You called here four times today alone. Give it a rest!" Then she hung up on me, ain't that somethin'?

All I'm tryin' to do is get Jerald's attention before somebody else grabs him. But his mama's got hold of the telephone so tight, I can't get to him. I can't see nothin' wrong with talkin' to Jerald on the phone—ain't her money payin' for it no way.

Well, Jerald's mama sees it different. Last night she actually called my house and talked to my father. (That's what I get for leavin' my name and number so Jerald could call me back.) Next thing I knew, Daddy was sittin' me down for a talk.

At first I was sure Daddy was gettin' ready to yell at me. But then I noticed he wasn't frownin', just sittin' there, real quiet. "I hear you like somebody named Jerald," he said.

I shrugged like it wasn't any big thing, me likin' Jerald. The way Daddy was actin', I wasn't sure what he meant.

"You ever wonder what they must be sayin' to each other when you all aren't around? I'm talkin' about Jerald and the other dudes you see around school and around where we live. I bet you'd like to know, wouldn't you? I'll let you in on a secret. You know what they say to each other when it's just men around, no women? When it comes to ladies who do all the

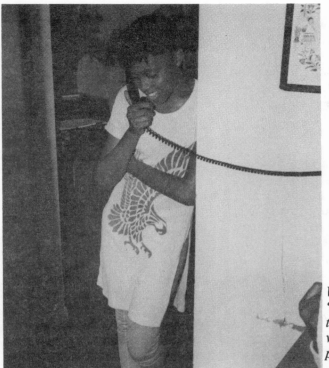

When she "burns up" the phone line, what's a parent to do?

callin', they talk about 'em the same way they talk about women who do all the payin'—the ones who got their hands in their pockets soon as they see a man comin'. Know what they say about ladies like that? They say, 'Man, I can get anything I want from 'em. I ain't even got to ask. Easy, man. Nothin' to it.'

"They think it's easy, Tina. They see ladies like that, they figure why should they act any different? Is that how you really want somebody to treat you—like you're an automatic cash machine?"

"I'm not givin' Jerald no money!" I exclaimed. "Got no money to give him anyway. Besides, everybody else I know does it that way. What's wrong with callin' Jerald?"

Daddy sighed. "Seems okay, don't it, callin' him on the phone so you can get his attention." I nodded; sure seemed all right to me. "But there's more to it than that. Don't you want to get to know him better, maybe go to the movies with him, spend time with him?" I nodded again; yeah, I figured me and Jerald were gonna get to more than phone conversations. "All that stuff takes time," Daddy continued. "It doesn't happen in a second, it hasn't happened just yet, and it's only going to happen if two people are in on it, not just you, but Jerald's got to be there too."

"Yeah, sure Daddy. But I don't get what you're sayin'. I'm just tryin' to make sure Jerald don't forget about me."

"Sweetness, if Jerald's dumb enough to forget about you, he's dumb enough for you to forget. Maybe if you try to remember how special you are, you'll be able to give things a chance to grow. If Jerald likes you, he'll return some of those calls you made. You made your play, now it's his turn."

Just to show you how serious Daddy was, he told me he'd promised Jerald's mama I wouldn't call there for at least a week and he expected me to keep that promise. He said if Jerald was interested, it wouldn't take him more than a week to get back to me. Daddy said he knew this from long experience at bein' a man. I guess I can't argue with that so I might as well give this a try. But three days have passed and there's been no call from Jerald. If I'm so special, how come Jerald's actin' like he hasn't noticed?

Mama says not to look so worried and to quit starin' at the telephone so much. She keeps tellin' me to remember what Daddy told me about not makin' everything so easy for a man. Well, I'm tryin' to keep it in mind, but it sure seems like bein' special puts you on the waitin' end.

One of the most frequently heard complaints from Black parents concerns the kind of behavior that "Tina" shows—her aggressive handling of her interest in "Jerald." Young Black females like "Tina," who are much more likely to initiate contact with their male peers, is an area of behavior that is distinctly different from the way in which adults treated each other when they were adolescents. In those days, male-female contact—whether at parties, in school, or around the neighborhood—tended to be started almost exclusively by males. It was the young man who asked a young woman to dance; a young woman almost never asked a young man for his telephone number, unless she'd known him for a long time; and a young woman was supposed to wait for a young man to show his interest in her—her interest in him was not the deciding factor in terms of who made the approach first.

But as "Tina" shows us, times have changed decisively. Young women no longer wait for young men; in fact, in many cases nowadays, adolescent females are quite aggressive about their approach toward adolescent males. Clearly, the changing roles of adult males and females have had their effect on our youth.

But to what degree is that effect having a productive impact on their development? This is a difficult question to answer, mainly because the roles of males and females are still in the process of changing. This is one of the reasons that the father in "Burning up the wires" tries not to be overly critical. He tries, instead, to put his daughter's aggressiveness in terms of balance. He points out that she's "made her play" and he implies he sees nothing really wrong with that. He also makes it clear that when Black women behave in an overly aggressive manner toward Black men, their relationship is not productive for either of them—one treats the other like an object ("an automatic cash machine") rather than a person. His discussion of how "the dudes talk" when women aren't around lets "Tina" in on the heart of the problem when one gender tips the balance in a relationship; being someone who's "easy" is contrasted with the struggle required to develop and maintain a fair and balanced male-female relationship.

This scenario, then, highlights one effective approach that Black parents can make when it comes to the issue of aggression in their adolescent daughters. It will probably do no good to lecture a daughter about how wrong it is to be "pushy." An approach like this will probably be confusing to her, given the dominant culture's images of aggressive women. She is likely to have seen many a television program and advertisement in which women initiate lots of contact in bars, parties, and bedrooms and men respond favorably. In that context, a young Black female doesn't see her behavior as aggressive; she's merely imitating what society has shown her to be acceptable behavior. Instead, when an adolescent daughter "burns up the wires" or otherwise shows aggression toward her male peers in social settings, an approach that keeps balance and fairness as the goal of relating to males, will allow her room to be assertive without being manipulative and domineering.

School is Not Free

"Ooh, you look so nice!" Letha exclaimed as her sister Donna walked into the living room.

Donna struck a pose while their mother grabbed the camera. "Donny, get out of the picture," she told her son. "Letha, go get the corsage from the refrigerator."

Letha pulled her younger brother out of camera range. "C'mon, Donny. Race you to the kitchen!"

Seconds later, Letha carefully held the corsage of orchid and baby's breath. It feels so soft and smells so sweet, she thought. If this were my corsage, I'd want to keep it forever. I'd put it in a glass box in my room and look at it every night. I'd . . .

"What're you doin'?" Donny asked. "You're lookin' at that stupid flower like you never seen one before! Hey, Ma!" he called, running down the hall. "Letha's been readin' too many books. She's gone nuts!"

"Shut up, boy. What do you know about nuts? C'mon, Letha, hurry up. I want to take some pictures with her corsage on before Earl gets here."

Sighing, Letha helped her mother pin the corsage on her sister's dress. "Honey, you really do look a sight to see," their mother declared as she wiped her eyes. "All that extra scrimpin' and savin' is come to pass—Letha, take some pictures, will you? I've got to find some tissues to put in Donna's purse."

Donna smiled in the camera's direction while Letha snapped the picture. "That's the third time today," Donna said. "Mama's been boo-hooin' like crazy! She did spend a pretty penny on this dress. Guess it makes her feel good to see me gettin' ready to graduate."

"We'll probably need a bucket at her feet at the graduation," said Donny.

Their laughter was interrupted by the sound of the doorbell. "That's Earl!" Donna exclaimed. She dashed to the bathroom to check her appearance, a few more pictures were taken of the couple, and everyone ran outside to wave Donna and Earl off.

"You'd think they was gettin' married or somethin'," Donny said as they came inside. "They're comin' back, ain't they?"

Letha slumped onto a chair. "Donny, you just don't understand. Maybe in a few more years, once you're in high school, then you'll start to get it. Senior prom—it's the biggest and best party you'll ever go to!"

Donny shrugged. "If you say so. Anyway, we don't have to worry about goin' through that again, not around this house."

Mrs. Carter began picking up empty film packages. "What're you talkin' about, Donny? Letha here's gonna be goin' in a couple of years."

"Letha? Ha!" her son replied. "Who's gonna take a bookworm like her? Ain't no dudes lined up to take her out now, how's she gonna get anybody to take her to a prom? Why, her glasses are so thick, she'd probably knock a dude blind when it came time to kiss him good night!"

Letha barely heard her brother's parting insult. She fled to her and Donna's bedroom and slammed the door. As a flood of tears smeared her glasses, she yanked them off her face. Stupid glasses, she thought. Stupid glasses, stupid Donny, stupid, stupid prom. Who cares about that stuff—not me, she decided. I don't have to go to a prom. I'm going to college to study chemistry so I can become a world famous chemist.

I'll just study harder, she told herself as she dried off her glasses and pushed them back on her nose. I'll study harder and longer, and maybe I'll get to graduate early—then it won't matter if I don't go to the prom. I'll already be in college while the rest of 'em will be at some stupid party.

"Can I come in, honey?" her mother asked.

Letha opened the door. "I'm fine, Mama. I was just getting ready to study for my chemistry exam."

Mrs. Carter sat on Donna's bed. "I want to talk to you first. Don't pay attention to Donny, you know he was just teasin' you."

Letha shook her head. "It's true, Mama. I'll probably break the record and be the only one at Carver High who goes all the way through school without one date."

"Well, I don't know why—you're just as pretty as Donna and you're twice as smart! Besides, you'll have plenty of time for goin' out, once you've reached your goal. You've got somethin' special, Letha, somethin' no date in this world can replace. I'm so proud of the way you hit those books—honey, you're one in a million! Donny's proud of you too, he's just too busy crackin' jokes to remember sometimes."

Letha hugged her mother. "Thanks, Mama. Don't worry. I'll be fine. I've got to study now."

Hours later, Letha shut her textbook and went to bed. As she lay staring at the ceiling, she imagined what her sister must be doing. By now she's probably at one of those after-sets she mentioned. Must be somethin', she thought, somethin' I'll never get to see. Well, if I'm gonna break the record and be "one in a million," I guess it's the price I have to pay to become a chemist, Letha decided as she drifted off to sleep.

In "School is Not Free," a young Black female confronts a struggle that many have to deal with. "Letha" is academically successful but she is not so successful when it comes to dating. In fact, she is dateless; worse still, she is pessimistic about her prospects of having any social life while she's in high school. Her brother calls her a "bookworm"—a term that has always conjured up the image of someone whose life is limited to scholarly matters. As "Letha" watches her older sister prepare for her senior prom, she believes it will not be an event that she will ever enjoy.

The struggle "Letha" faces, in which she experiences conflict between what she is and what she's been led to believe she should be, is known as anomie. Anomie, as explained by Robert Merton in 1949, occurs when someone looks for alternative ways of coping because society does not or will not provide ways for reaching goals such as getting an education, finding employment, etc. Merton pointed to five ways in which anomie takes place; out of these, Jo-Ellen Asbury named four which she believes are particularly relevant for Black people when it comes to involvement in violence:

1. Innovation: Finding alternative means of achieving the same cultural goals.

2. Ritualism: Diminishing aspirations to a point at which the individual can attain the goals.

3. Retreatism: Complete withdrawal from cultural goals and aspirations.

4. Rebellion: Seeking to replace cultural goals with a new social structure.[9]

"Letha" enjoys academic pursuit; she is especially interested in learning as much as she can about chemistry. Yet her conflict becomes increasingly strong because she's aware that many of her peers are involved in other interests such as dating and developing relationships with the opposite sex. She's been led to believe that "bookworms" can't be popular socially and that the price she'll have to pay for her academic focus will be a dateless adolescence. Within her world as she sees it, "Letha's" ways of achieving her goals and interests in chemistry aren't acceptable. To "Letha," her scholarly interests are contrary to popularity and acceptance among her peers.

So "Letha" struggles to find an alternative way of life. She decides that she should skip a social life, at least for now. She prefers to continue her academic focus, because she believes this concentration will get her what she wants—to become a chemist. Although she is wistful about the fun she is missing, "Letha" is determined to pursue her goal. In the realm of anomie, "Letha" is using the strategy of "rebellion." She seeks to replace the social environment (as she sees it) with a different structure—in spite of what others might call her, she organizes and spends her time in ways that will complement her academic interest and goal.

Although "Letha" is wise to pursue her life with determination and an eye toward her future, her "rebellion" may not be as necessary as she perceives it. True, many people—young and old—tend to ridicule those for whom academics are enjoyable. Many a high school has its share of students who assume that "bookworms" don't want a social life. However, there are also schools in which academically successful students are also socially popular—they have plenty of dates, they get along well with not-so-successful students, and their lives are well-integrated with a variety of activities. In short, it is quite possible to break the stereotyped image of a "bookworm" and be a well-rounded young Black female.

Part of what may be causing someone like "Letha" to experience a conflict like anomie is rooted in her self-image. As was mentioned in Chapter One, during adolescence, a female often feels insecure about her self-image. Because she wears thick eyeglasses, this may contribute to any lack of confidence she feels. In addition, there may be a "herd instinct" at her school which implies that a "bookworm" can't be popular; if so, this may certainly reinforce the insecurity she's struggling to deal with. And of course, family members can affect an adolescent's self-image and "Donny" has indicated his belief in the stereotype of the "bookworm." All these factors contribute to the development and support of a young Black female's self-image.

With this situation, we can examine how academic pursuits operate in a diverse context. There are many possible factors that influence the degree to which Black adolescent females focus on school as an avenue to their future. The quality of the teaching staff, access to supplies and equipment, the administrators' attitude, availability of extra-curricular programs, and the classes offered all play their role in contributing to academic success or failure among students. Just as important, though, are the *attitudes* of students, faculty and parents toward learning. As the struggle of "Letha" points out, when there are attitudes among people that place academically successful adolescents in a bind—where they supposedly must choose between books and dates—it becomes very difficult for students to get serious about academics without feeling like failures in the other aspects of their lives.

That's why it was so important for "Letha's" mother to comfort her daughter and be supportive of her goals and interests. True to her nature and that of so many other Black mothers, she does just that; she insists that "Letha" is not unattractive and even moreso, she promotes the idea that being smart is attractive in itself. She points out how proud she is of her daughter, and she encourages "Letha" to keep the long-term view in mind. This is one of the biggest reasons that Black youth, male and female, succeed in pursuing their goals—they have the undying love and encouragement of their parents.

The Rap

"Well, I still don't see why I can't go. I already bought my ticket and I used my own money to pay for it. I work hard at that job to get some money, and I've been savin' a lot of what I get, so it's not like I'm runnin' around wastin' my check every week. And here I get a chance to use a little of my own money to go to a concert, and you tell me you don't like the music?! That's not a good reason—so what if you don't like rappers? What's that got to do with anything?"

Benetha Miller shook her head. Her daughter was giving her a headache. "Rappers—what's so great about them?" she asked. "I think it's a waste of your hard-earned money. Besides, you went out and bought that ticket without asking me first. You may be 16 and got yourself a job on the weekends, but you ain't grown yet, young lady."

"Okay, so I should've asked you first," Cheryl admitted. "At the time I didn't think you'd say no. It's not like this is the first time I've ever gone to a concert. And you know I listen to rap—I got lots of tapes around here."

"Hmph, another waste of money. Well, I guess I can't keep you from spending some of your money on junk like rap music, but I sure am not gonna let you go to that concert! Now you listen to me, Cheryl, and listen good. I've got one big reason why you've got no business goin' to nobody's rap concert. You may not pay attention to what's bein' said on the news, but I do. I've been listening to what's been happenin' at those concerts. There's been gangbangers at just about every one of those concerts, and the police ain't been able to stop them from gettin' out of control—bustin' heads, shootin', gettin' the crowd all worked up. You're not to have any part of that, I can't take that chance, no ma'am."

"But Mama, rappers don't have a thing to do with that. It's not their fault that stuff happens at their concerts. Please Mama, I promise I'll be careful. I'm goin' with three other people and none of 'em are gangbangers. You know I wouldn't hang around with gangbangers. Please Mama," Cheryl pleaded.

Her mother shook her head firmly. "I said no and that's what I meant. You'll just have to sell your ticket to somebody foolish enough to risk their life so they can go listen to some ole funky rap music."

Cheryl stomped out of the apartment. "Funky ole rap music," her mother called it. She's really bein' unfair, Cheryl thought angrily. How's she know it's gonna be dangerous at this rap concert? The way she's talkin', you'd think rappers ran around actin' like criminals. She doesn't even listen to rap music. Every time I play one, she tells me to put my headphones on 'cause she can't stand to hear it. Why should I listen to her when she won't listen to anything I like? Cheryl kicked the fence surrounding her apartment building. I sure wish I was old enough to go where I please without no mama to always stop me, she thought.

Music has always meant good news and bad news between parents and their children. It seems there is no contemporary generation in America where there hasn't been disagreement between parents and children. Perhaps, then, music should be kept in perspective; after all, there will probably always be differences in musical tastes—that's partly why there are so many musical styles recorded and played.

In the "Miller" household, the particular disagreement about music centers on rap, a style that is recent enough to be beyond the adolescence of "Benetha Miller." But more than surface difference has emerged in this situation. Rap music, both in content and in the appearance and attitude of its performers, tends to be "street" music. It originated among performers whose style of dress and choice of words has clearly made them part of the street culture that is the environment of thousands of Black youth. Rap music is distinctly separate from the dominant culture's images, especially those that point to the upwardly mobile, middle class world. Consequently, rap is popular among many Black youth whose lives parallel what is said in rap and by whom it is performed. In addition, rap is imitated by dozens of would-be, adolescent rappers on street corners and at house parties.

Unfortunately, rap has recently come to be connected with the negative elements of street culture. I say recently because rap music did not begin that way; only since about 1987 have rap concerts experienced gang problems. In addition, as "Cheryl" points out, rappers themselves have made it clear that they don't condone gang involvement or violence. In fact, a close listen to various rap records will tell anyone that the words have a positive message about many critical issues affecting Black youth today: fighting drug use, developing racial pride, and preventing pregnancy are among the topics covered in these songs. So whatever gang problems that have occurred at rap concerts may be more a case of renewed gang involvement among Black youth which appears at these concerts because of the age group in the audience.

But "Benetha Miller" doesn't see it that way. She criticizes rap music and its fans, and she refuses to allow her daughter a legitimate choice in musical taste. In fact, she won't give rap music any credibility; she calls it "a waste of hard-earned money." This kind of attitude on the part of parents forces a gap between them and daughters like "Cheryl" which does little to promote or sustain communication and mutual respect.

It is understandable that a mother like "Benetha Miller" would hesitate to allow her daughter to be in a risky situation. Certainly, it is possible that "Cheryl" might encounter danger if the rap concert is also attended by warring gang members. "Cheryl" would be more understanding of her mother's refusal if it is grounded in terms of safety without the accompanying criticism of her musical preference.

When it comes to Black people, there's a lot of good news about music. The lengthy careers of many Black performers provide great potential for common appreciation and interest between generations. When you think of people like Gladys Knight and the Pips, Smokey Robinson, and many other Black performers, it's easy to see how parents and their adolescent offspring might well be listening to some of the same records. In addition, nowadays there are emerging similarities between musical styles and greater air time being given to some styles that previously received a lot less air play. I'm speaking now of what has been loosely called "jazz" and has been influenced by other styles such as "fusion" and "rhythm and blues." Black jazz musicians like Grover

Washington, Jr. were rarely heard on the radio stations frequented by youth, but much change has occurred and it's now possible for Black adolescents to become acquainted with music that used to be unfamiliar to them. And performers like Stevie Wonder represent a style that any age group enjoys. One of the strengths of Black music, then, is its cross-generational appeal.

Hopefully, the rap scenario will remind Black parents that disagreements about music don't have to become starting points for battles with their adolescent daughters. There will always be some amount of individual difference about musical preferences. In addition, it is certainly a parent's responsibility to make sure her or his daughter's musical enjoyment isn't blemished by neighborhood influences like gangs. However, music is also an opportunity for families to find common ways to spend time together, appreciating one of our strongest, most durable traditions. The value of music for Black families is in its ability to draw people together for mutual pleasure.

Friday Night Fight

Oh no, Janetha Billings thought as she saw her daughter slip from her bedroom to the bathroom. Round 68 of the Billings' Friday night fights.

"Jim," she called to her husband.

"Hmmm?" he answered absentmindedly.

She walked into the living room and turned off the basketball game her husband was watching. "We have to talk. Dalila's about to get picked up for that party..."

"I know, I know. I already said she could go. Now, the game's in the third quarter..."

"Forget the game, Jim. She's heading out of here with . . ."

The doorbell rang and Mrs. Billings went to answer it. She ushered three of Dalila's friends into the living room, then went back to her daughter's room. I can't let her out of this house with that outfit on, she thought. We'll just have to fight, that's all.

"Well, I gotta go," Dalila said as she rushed toward her bedroom door.

"Not with that on, you won't," her mother said, blocking her path. "You go right back to your closet and keep pulling out clothes until you find something I say is okay to wear!"

Dalila's face crinkled up as though she was about to cry. "But, Mama . . ."

Mrs. Billings shook her head firmly. "No buts. Do it now, Dalila."

Several minutes later, Jim Billings knocked on his daughter's door. "What's going on in there? Dalila's keeping her guests waiting. What's taking so long?"

His wife let him in. "Dalila's not going to the party. She says she has nothing to wear," Mrs. Billings proclaimed, pointing to the pile of clothes on Dalila's bed.

"Daddy, she's bein' so mean to me! She won't let me wear what I want to wear, and this stuff is what I wear to school or church, not to a party!" she exclaimed angrily.

"Is this what you were gonna wear to the party?" he demanded as he picked up a mini-dress lying on a chair. "Girl, this dress wouldn't cover you when you were 10, let alone now. Did you buy this thing when you went shopping with Carlotta last week?"

Dalila nodded, her lower lip trembling. "What's wrong with it? Everybody's wearing minis."

"Not everybody, honey," her mother said quietly. "It just seems that way. *You're* not wearing them and you're not going out of here with that dress on. There are plenty of other clothes here . . ."

"Who cares about that stuff?" Dalila yelled. "How come I have to walk around looking like some nerd! You get to wear what you want—you and Daddy go out looking nice, why can't I? Just last weekend, you had on some tight leather pants and a top that was cut down to *here*—how come that's okay?"

"That's different and you know it!" her father yelled. "And while you're at it, you can go to the bathroom and wash off all that make-up. Janetha, look at her—she's got on so much red lipstick, she looks like a clown!"

Dalila ran to the bathroom and slammed the door. She turned the faucet on full, hoping the sound of the water would hide her crying. She glanced around for a washcloth. Look at all this stuff, she thought. Containers of foundation, eye shadow, moisturizer, men's cologne, nail polish, and eye liner filled the shelves and countertop. "Do as I say and not as I do," that's what her parents constantly told her. It makes me sick, Dalila decided bitterly.

Clothes and cosmetics represent particular challenges in relationships between Black parents and their adolescent daughters. During this stage of their daughters' growth,

45

these two issues often become the source of great disagreement. To the parents, clothing styles frequently become ways of measuring self-respect and good values. To the daughters, clothing can become a way of showing maturity and belonging to a peer group's standards of dress. In addition, adolescent females, it should be remembered, are preoccupied with their self-image. They badly want to "look good"—not in their parents' eyes, but in the eyes of their peers. They also want to stop looking like children; in many cases, what they wore just a year or two ago is no longer desirable from their viewpoint.

Cosmetics is combined in this situation with clothes because it often is paired with clothing in parent-daughter confrontations. Make-up is a symbol that adolescent females use to make themselves look and feel more grown-up. As young children, these same females might have played with make-up when they played "house." Now they're more serious about cosmetics; to them, eye shadow, lipstick and all the other cosmetic items are part of their "tool kit" to bring them a more womanly appearance. In addition—although there might be many brothers who would disagree—the prevailing notion is that make-up somehow improves a woman's appearance and thereby gives her a better chance of attracting the opposite sex. Consequently, with clothes and cosmetics, adolescent females feel more confident about their self-image and their sexuality.

However, the scenario highlights the difficulty parents have with handling clothes and cosmetics. It would be simple for the "Billings" to treat clothes and make-up as just their daughter's natural tendency to be an adolescent. She's just going through a phase, this viewpoint argues, why get so upset about it? She'll get over her preoccupation with "wild" styles like mini-dresses and her overly applied lipstick. Besides, what parent hasn't had some kind of disagreement with his or her child about clothing styles?

Among Black families, arguments about clothing and cosmetics have another level of meaning. When parents get extremely upset about styles of dress worn by their daughters, they are partly battling stereotyped images of Black females. The "Jezebel" stereotype comes particularly to mind. "Jezebel," that depreciated sex object, has often been shown in books, movies and television programs as a prostitute dressed in tight, short, skirts or dresses and wearing thick applications of make-up (including red lipstick). So "Janetha" and "Jim" looked at "Dalila" and on a subconscious or conscious level, they saw "Jezebel." No matter how fashionable styles like mini-dresses might be, part of their disapproval is rooted in a disavowal of "Jezebel" as an acceptable image for their daughter to imitate.

On the other hand, "Dalila" has a point to make. She mentions that her mother has been known to dress seductively, and she angrily notices all the cosmetic items in their bathroom. Thus "Dalila" recognizes some inconsistency; she is haunted by her parents' often repeated byword, "Do as I say and not as I do." This segment of the scenario can be the most difficult and frustrating challenge confronted by parents and daughters. Adolescents can be quite sophisticated and sensitive; they're often much more aware of inconsistencies than adults give them credit for being. From an adolescent's point of view, if she's to pay attention and absorb the knowledge to be provided by a parent, it can be tough going if a parent isn't following the same advice.

My intention here is not so much to "lecture" parents about their own sense of fashion and beauty. Experience has taught me that the road to appreciating one's outward appearance and natural beauty is a path that each person must take in her own way and time. What is important to point out, though, is that an adolescent female will often "teach" a parent more than might have been expected. "Dalila" is letting us all know that, if she's to develop her own sense of fashion, she will be fighting a "herd instinct" that is beyond her age group. There are plenty of adults—Black and Caucasian, male and female — who have a lot to learn before they can say they are free from blindly following this week's fads about make-up and clothing. Since many of those adults are also parents of adolescent females, what they're trapped by will affect how they deal with cosmetics and dress styles in their offspring.

Therefore, each side is right in some way in the "Billings" situation. "Jim" and "Janetha" are correct to protest their daughter's manner of dressing. As a matter of fact, the situation presents an effective opportunity to point out the "Jezebel" stereotype as a major source of their disapproval. "Dalila" is also correct about her disagreement when she emphasizes the inconsistency between what her parents are saying and how they're behaving. Does this mean that "Janetha" should never wear leather or make-up? Not necessarily; there may be some additional garments—such as a mid-calf tunic

—that would lend an image more distant from "Jezebel." And make-up itself doesn't have to be a bad thing; after all, some of our African foresisters—such as Egyptian women—were renowned for their finesse with cosmetics. The idea overall, whether it's clothing or cosmetics, is one of balance and moderation; used appropriately and with an individual awareness of its enhancing effects, dress and make-up can show the world the highlights of a woman's self-image.

Cosmetics and clothing are actually opportunities for parents and daughters to collaborate. Together they can: learn how to tell a well-made garment from one that will probably fall apart soon; hunt for bargains that are not only low-cost but long-lasting; sew clothing and include unique touches that will make a garment designer quality; stimulate ideas in an adolescent for possible career choices and ways to make money now; and reinforce an area of domestic responsibility that will last her a lifetime. Cosmetics can be treated similarly: many items on the market—such as face masks and hair products—can be made at home, using foods such as oatmeal and lemon juice. (There are books which explain how to do this; they can be found at libraries, bookstores and natural food shops.) In addition, by hunting around in places like natural food stores, some cosmetics can be purchased which are more beneficial to young skin because they don't contain additives and other synthetic by-products. Overall, alternatives are important to use with Black adolescent females because they give her a broader view of what is possible when it comes to projecting her self-image. She needs these alternatives as part of the tools she can use to combat stereotyped images and to nurture an image that will reinforce her self-esteem.

You Talk Too Much

Rahsaan Barrington reached for the pile of bills and began opening them. "What time are we supposed to meet Aziza and Kofi?" he asked his wife.

"In a little over an hour," Rita Barrington replied as she glanced at the wall clock. She turned the page of a book she was reading. "We'd better start getting ready."

"Yeah, *you'd* better start. You know you always take twice as long as I do, what with all the times you change your mind about.... What in the...?" He stared at the phone bill in disbelief.

"What's the matter?" his wife asked. She looked over his

shoulder while he jabbed at the total on the bill. "There must be some mistake, that can't be our bill—that's over $200 in local calls!" she exclaimed.

Her husband shook his head. "I don't understand. It can't be you or me—with us both having to travel so much, we're barely here. And your mama isn't one to talk on the phone. So it's gotta be . . ."

His wife nodded. "You got it. Malika and Masani."

Rahsaan gritted his teeth. "We've got to have a talk with our daughters. We're not working ourselves this hard to pay for this mess. Things are going to change around here right now!"

"I think it's time for some *real* changes, Rahsaan. Let's look at the whole picture. You know how we've been saying we're away too much?" she asked.

"We sure are—if we were home a little more, we'd never have let them stay on the phone so much. We'll just have to try to rearrange our work schedules so at least one of us is here more often. I think we need to take the phone out of the twins' room, too. They don't need access to the phone if they're going to misuse it," he declared.

"That makes me think of something else we need to work on," his wife stated. "Misuse—the girls aren't using their time at home like they need to. Masani and Malika are 13, it's way past time they started taking on more of the housework than just cleaning their room. Mama spoils them, and we let her."

Her husband nodded firmly. "When we get back from dinner, we'll make up a schedule. You're right, Rita. It's time for some real changes around here!"

"Get up, 'lika! We'll be late for dance class," Masani said as she nudged her sister the next morning.

"Good morning. We have some special announcements for you," the girls' mother said as they sat down for breakfast.

"This is your new schedule, ladies." Rahsaan placed two sheets of paper on the table. "From now on, we're all going to get involved in the running of this household. Now, don't worry about time for homework—your mother and I have put that in your schedules. And your dance class is in there too. We've divided up the chores that me, your mama and your grandmother used to do without your help, and that means cooking, cleaning, washing clothes, taking out the garbage, grocery shopping —the whole bit. We'll be right there to show you how to do all the housework you need to learn."

"Oh, and be sure you pay close attention to *this*," their mother said, pointing to one small square on the schedule.

" 'Telephone time,' " Malika read. " 'Fifteen minutes'—a week?!" she exclaimed.

"That's correct, young lady," her mother replied. "Fifteen minutes per week, and that's exactly what it means. We think we're being very reasonable, especially when you consider the phone bill we just got. Your father and I are not going to tolerate any more $200 phone bills—we're not working as hard as we work to pay for you and Masani to talk on the phone for hours. As a matter of fact, we've decided your allowances are going to pay for half of that last bill. So you won't be getting any money for the next few months."

"Okay, we can see why you'd want to do that, right 'lika?" Masani said as her sister nodded quickly. "But why the schedule? Is that more punishment? I mean, we won't do it again. We'll stay off the phone the whole time we're off allowance."

Her father smiled. He could see his daughters didn't get the point. "Listen, my children. We want you to know something important. Your mother and I have had busy jobs and we thought if we worked real hard, we'd be doing what's best for you by giving you a good life. Well, we've done pretty good as far as money's concerned—you've got all the things any girls' parents could buy you."

"But there's more to a good life than things," his wife continued. "You two are old enough to start learning what your father and I understand better than all the money we've ever made —how to run a household. I know it sounds boring and terrible, like punishment. But it's not. Why, what would this place be like if we had all the money in the world but we didn't know how to cook and clean?" she asked.

Malika shrugged. "You'd just hire a maid and a cook," she said. "That's how they do it on TV."

Her father sighed. "Rita," he told his wife, "we've got a lot of work to do."

In today's world of frozen dinners, microwave ovens, and fast food restaurants, domestic responsibility has generally tended to get "swept under the carpet" when it comes to adolescent development. Has the traditional image, of the Black mother teaching her daughter the ins and outs of running a home, gone by the wayside? What about the more immediate needs in some Black families for the adolescent female sibling to be a secondary "mother" for her brothers and younger sisters? Are male and female siblings handling their end of the household chores, or are sisters the primary children bearing the brunt of the duties?

The scenario of the "Barrington" family emphasizes the need to consciously develop domesticity among adolescent females. This is partly true because there are so many conveniences available nowadays—in the form of equipment or products—that someone or something is frequently "doing" what a person relied on herself to do before. It is no longer necessary to stand over a pot and shake it to make popcorn; an automatic popcorn popper will now do that for you (and at an affordable price). Why should someone spend hours cooking a meal when meals from fast food places have become varied and inexpensive enough to make convenient options. What's the point of knowing how to scrub clothes by hand, make a hand-sewn dress, darn a hole in a sock, or dye a T-shirt— machines can handle all those tasks faster than any human ever could. Besides, items can be replaced more easily than they could ever be handmade.

Technological advances promise the prospect of more automation in our lives, not less. There may well be the day within our lifetimes, when craftsmakers become an endangered species, machines really are doing all our housework for us, and children grow up without ever knowing what a "home-cooked meal" tastes like. Am I exaggerating? I hope so; if we do reach this lifestyle as a nation, we will be doing our children a great disservice.

Before I give you the idea that I have returned to nature and have no contact with technology, let me clarify myself. This is not an attempt to make technology appear to be an evil god to which we're all enslaved. Rather, in the realm of adolescent development, domestic responsibilities carry a critical opportunity for parents to grasp. Just as the "Barringtons" realized, when a child reaches adolescence, it's time to prepare her for her future as an adult. Part of her future will include the very day-to-day tasks that parents might be doing for her but she will have to do herself. So there's a practical consideration to deal with when it comes to domestic responsibilities. Obviously, if she's to become a self-sufficient adult, she's going to need to know about cooking, cleaning, grocery shopping, budgeting, laundry, etc. It would be highly impractical to assume that she'll quickly be so awash in cash that she can hire someone else to do those things for her—anyone who's tried to exist on frozen dinners every day will tell you how much money is being wasted versus buying raw food to cook.

On another level, the notion of domesticity has even more meaning here. Being rooted in one's own home—domesticity —is an often overlooked idea when it comes to adolescent development. Perhaps because it's right there to be explored, domesticity is ignored by many adults who are involved every day with adolescents. Still, this idea is rich with possibilities and deserves further examination.

To be domestic is to be connected to the duties and pleasures of the home and family. Clearly, a definition like this opens the door for a refreshed view of domesticity, the quality of being domestic. If an adolescent Black female learns to be connected to pleasures and duties of the home and family, she approaches her family relationships quite differently than someone who sees domesticity only as boring, punishing work. The home and family are not enemies to avoid, but a welcome refuge peopled by familiar loved ones. Domesticity represents an opportunity to encourage an attitude toward home life that will nurture young Black females' lives presently and in the future.

I am aware that Black homes and families exist in which domestic violence and impoverished circumstances greatly limit the degree to which these settings and people can mean a refuge for a Black adolescent female. I also believe that part of what may prevent her from having a home like that in her future will mean a different frame of reference regarding domesticity.

What might such a frame of reference include? Since domestic means "duties and pleasures of the home and family," it will certainly embrace a variety of activities. I would also advocate a balancing of activity types so as to give adolescent daughters chances to learn different skills. Therefore, the "Barringtons'" idea of making up schedules is an effective one; it allows the parents to take into account time needed for homework or any other obligations not related to housework. A schedule also helps parents to see the whole picture so they can shift tasks from one offspring to another, from week to week or month to month. Finally, a schedule helps parents see where they fit in; there may be occasions when an adolescent needs a parent's guidance or instruction the first few times, particularly with certain tasks—pleasurable or dutiful—such as changing oil in a car, batiking a T-shirt, babysitting, making a quilt, etc.

The situation with the "Barringtons" began with a conflict over the telephone. I used the telephone in this situation because domesticity involves the use of time, as "Rita" wisely pointed out. When parents do not fully grasp the significance of domestic responsibilities, time spent at home needs filling in other ways; naturally, adolescent females will fill a great deal of it on the telephone unless otherwise stimulated or instructed. And when domesticity enters a family's viewpoint toward themselves and their home, time spent at home is anticipated, not dreaded—the telephone loses its domination in a teenager's world.

As for Black families, there is a particular issue at stake regarding domesticity. At first glance, it might appear that there is no issue to argue; aren't Black daughters heavily trained in domestic duties? Certainly, they once were; one of a Black mother's areas of authority over which she had control and expertise was in the domestic training of her daughter.

But some recent changes have had some effect on this issue. First, there is the changing role of males and females as it relates to duties in the home; in this realm, it should be pointed out that Black males have also taken part in domestic duties; Robert Staples was among those who made this clear, in his book *Black Masculinity*. So females are far from being the only ones in Black families who know how to run a household. That is why I continually emphasized that each "Barrington" parent took part in domestic duties. Second, the degree to which Black adolescent females receive domestic training depends partly on their parents' availability to provide the instruction. If parents become so preoccupied with their careers and the other aspects of their own lives, they can spend relatively little time helping their children learn how to run and enjoy home life. Third, how much adolescent Black females view domesticity as a natural part of their development will have a tremendous effect on their lives as adults. In other words, if roots to her home and family are encouraged and deepened, as an adult she will seek to use her time to enhance and reinforce her home and family life. This will help her make choices and decisions that complement domesticity, not endanger it. The issue at stake, then, is whether Black parents view domesticity as a priority in their adolescent daughters' development; if they do, domestic responsibilities provide critical training points to encourage.

What Wade Nobles referred to as "the survival of the tribe"[10] demands that domesticity be taken into account. Whether a Black female marries, has children, or remains single and childless throughout her life, she will need to appreciate and sustain the duties and pleasures of home and family. If her home is to be her abiding shelter, she will surround it with the particular values and people that reinforce self-esteem and love. And at whatever level she views the notion of family—whether that be in the form of husband and children, husband only, or relatives such as siblings and cousins—her domesticity will enhance her view of familyhood. Domesticity can be a vehicle through which an adolescent Black female experiences day-to-day life in a satisfying, proactive manner. Through domesticity, young Black females can use the strategy of "rebellion" to replace the dominant culture's view of domestic duties as being mere drudgery, with a new social structure that in turn strengthens Black family life.

Nosy Neighbors?

It was almost midnight, and Tamara Jackson was upset. Her 15-year-old daughter Gloria was supposed to have been home an hour ago, and she'd always given Gloria clear instructions to call if anything was keeping her from being home on time. Mrs. Jackson looked at the clock again. What's happened, she asked herself. I wonder if it's got anything to do with what Mrs. Thompson told me about those kids she's been hanging around lately. There's something about them I don't really like, and when Gloria gets here . . .

The sound of a key in the apartment's front door interrupted her thoughts. The floorboards creaked as Gloria tiptoed down the hallway. "Hmph," Mrs. Jackson mumbled as she pushed the remote control button to turn off the television. "And just where do you think you're sneaking off to?"

"Hi, Mama." Here it comes, Gloria thought. She grabbed the nearest chair to steady herself.

"Sit down. I want to talk to you. Unh, unh, girl—right here," Gloria's mother commanded, patting the spot on the couch next to her.

Gloria moved slowly toward the couch. She rubbed her eyes and blinked. Everything's so blurred, she realized as she slid onto the couch.

Mrs. Jackson looked closely at her daughter. "So. What Mrs. Thompson told me about those friends of yours is true."

"Huh? What?" Gloria mumbled. *If I could just see clearly maybe I could hear what Mama's sayin',* she thought.

"Look at you." Mrs. Jackson shook her head and stood up, pulling her daughter by the arm. "Come on, you're comin' with me so you can get a good look at yourself." She pulled her daughter into the bathroom. For several minutes she doused Gloria with stinging, cold water. Then she held her wet, make-up smeared face under the sharp glare of the light.

"There," she shouted, pointing to Gloria's reflection in the mirror, "that's what your so-called 'friends' have done for you! How do you like yourself now?"

"Mama," Gloria whimpered as she turned away, "I'm gonna be sick. Please. . ."

It seemed to mother and daughter that hours passed before they were able to talk quietly to each other. Gloria's vomiting was followed by uncontrolled sobbing and through it all, her mother tumbled from fury to despair—yelling, wailing, grabbing Gloria as though she hoped she might squeeze her into guaranteeing she'd never come home high again. Now, as they sat curled on the couch sharing a blanket, they were too exhausted to fight anymore.

"What did Mrs. Thompson tell you?" Gloria asked hoarsely.

"I never should've let you hang around them. She warned me. She said, 'Honey, them's some no good kids. I seen 'em—drinkin' and fillin' the air with those reefers—right over at that vacant lot in broad daylight.' But I wouldn't listen to her. I figured I raised my baby not to do anything like drink or smoke—she *knows better*. This is my fault as much as it is yours. I should've paid closer attention."

Gloria hung her head. "I always thought she was just a nosy neighbor, gettin' in everybody's business."

Her mother put her arm around her shoulder. "So did I, honey. That's the mistake I made about her. But thank God for nosy neighbors like Mrs. Thompson. She's just what we both need!"

One of the terrors parents have is that their children will use drugs. Curiously, many parents are just beginning to see alcohol with the same concern. For too long, alcohol has been widely acceptable; in fact, it has been a kind of twisted "rite of passage" for adolescents—you're seen as "grown-up" if you can hold your liquor. Only recently have there been substantial efforts made to be realistic about the risks involved with alcohol consumption.

Now that alcohol can be realistically viewed alongside drugs like marijuana, heroin and cocaine, a situation like the one faced by the "Jacksons" can be examined and understood more effectively. The combined use of alcohol and marijuana was meant to demonstrate what frequently occurs; adolescents, when they get involved in substances like these, often consume them in combination. As was pointed out in a recent report by the Alcohol, Drug Abuse, and Mental Health Administration of the U.S. Public Health Service, the public should keep in mind that individual drugs are frequently consumed in combination with other drugs. Because of this, data about drug and alcohol abuse is tricky to measure; adverse consequences, for instance, may be known about one or two substances but not necessarily about various combinations of substances.

Nevertheless, it can be stated here that drug and alcohol consumption by Black people is still at a high level. According to the same report from the U.S. Public Health Service, emergency room episodes for cocaine use by Black patients increased from 378 cases in 564 health facilities in 1976, to 4,317 emergency room appearances by Black patients in 1986. Among 62 of the health facilities in the study, the three top-ranked substances accounting for drug-related deaths in the general population were alcohol-in-combination with other substances, heroin, and cocaine (in that order).[11]

Obviously, alcohol and drug consumption by adolescents should be avoided. While this statement may seem to some adults to be an obvious one, it bears mentioning nonetheless. (I am also not speaking here about prescription medication.) "Teaching" adolescents to use marijuana or drink alcoholic beverages in a "responsible" manner gives them a mixed message that endangers their ability to cope with life's ongoing challenges without needing a drink or a joint to feel all right. The difficulty with this issue for many parents is experienced when they themselves drink or consume drugs. It is one thing to sustain a clear belief against drugs and alcohol; but it is quite another matter to advise an adolescent against alcohol or drug consumption when a parent isn't following that advice. So while some parents may believe the solution is to teach responsible drinking for instance, this may only lead to more questions and conflict between themselves and their adolescents.

It is understandable, then, that "Tamara Jackson" reacts with a combination of rage and despair when she realizes her daughter is high. She is furious that "Gloria" would break what she thought was a well-understood rule about drug/alcohol consumption. She is also angry at herself for letting her daughter have contact with a peer group that will place her into conflict with her mother's values. "Tamara Jackson's" despair is rooted in her fear that "Gloria" will continue her current behavior; witnessing her daughter's behavior causes "Tamara" a deep sadness as well because she cannot help but feel a certain amount of failure in her responsibility as a mother.

But like so many other Black mothers, "Tamara" moves quickly and decisively to counteract what has happened. She wants to confront "Gloria" with the ugliness of alcohol and drug use so her daughter might contrast it with the seductive attraction these substances often hold for young people. She is also quick to realize the importance of "nosy neighbors" like "Mrs. Thompson."

So often in the past, Blacks have been able to prevent self-destructive tendencies among young people because we have a "community of watchers" around us, extending a network of reinforcement. "Mrs. Thompson" represents such a community, and it must be just such neighbors on whom Black people must depend for continuing to reinforce productive values. "Tamara Jackson" is thankful for her "nosy neighbor," and it appears that "Gloria" might be too. Apparently, "Gloria" has some level of recognition—through the cold confrontation in the bathroom—that drugs and alcohol will not contribute to developing her self-esteem. She also seems to realize that she needs neighbors like "Mrs. Thompson" to help her make appropriate choices when it comes to peer friendships. "Tamara Jackson" and her daughter cannot fight the influence of drugs and alcohol by themselves; all of us have a responsibility to lend our alertness and support to young Black females.

I found my place

Soubretta, age 16

Have you ever wanted to belong to something so you could feel all right about yourself? I used to feel that way about school, at least until I transferred.

Up until this school year, I went to a different high school than the one I attend now. The school was pretty good; some of the teachers encouraged me to study hard, and a couple of them gave me extra assignments. I was glad to get the work —I like school, no matter what anybody says. But the school I went to had a lot of problems. There were never enough supplies in the labs, a lot of teachers acted like they didn't care about teaching, and too many kids were either walking around like zombies or disrupting classes all the time. I was really getting sick of it, and so were my parents.

Things began to change when a slot opened up and I transferred to this school. I'd been on a waiting list for three years and finally I was able to get in. Right away, I could tell things were going to be different. The halls are quieter, the students act like they want to be here, and all the teachers I've met are enthusiastic. It makes me feel like it was worth the wait.

Not that it's been easy. Making the transfer has meant I have to travel farther because my old school was closer to home. And I've had to spend more time studying because the classes are harder. I don't get to see my friends from the other school like I used to, and making friends is hard for me—I guess I'm kind of shy. Sometimes I miss my old school just because I knew it a lot better than my new school.

But a couple of things happened that have really made me feel good. The other day when I was in one of my classes, we were having a discussion about the civil rights movement. The teacher asked us to name at least three ways we could tell the movement made a difference in our own lives. Lots of kids said things like, "more jobs for Blacks," "voting rights," and "more Blacks elected to office." Like I said, I'm shy; it takes me a while to open up. But what the teacher asked us made me think about something and before I knew it, I was speaking up.

"I can't think of three things right now, but one thing I've noticed is right here at this school. I think the civil rights movement has helped us have an all-Black school where we can all be proud."

The teacher nodded slowly and smiled. "How has the civil rights movement helped us do that, Soubretta?" he asked.

I thought about it for a minute. It had to do with something my parents had told me a while ago, when they explained how they had participated in marches. "Well, Mr. Taylor," I began, "it's like my folks told me. When you fight for equality, you aren't fighting to be the same as everybody else. You're fighting for a chance to be the best people possible—equal to excellence, that's what they always told me. And here, I feel like I can reach that goal."

You know what happened? People started clapping and saying, "Sounds good to me," and Mr. Taylor wrote "Equal to Excellence" on the board. He said I'd made his day! To think that I made a teacher's day—I'd never even thought of it that way before.

Then something even better happened. Word came in the mail that I'd been accepted into the National Honor Society! I knew I'd been studying hard and getting good grades, but I hadn't paid much attention to anything else.

Turns out there's an Honors Club at my new school, and now I'm in it. The rest of the members are really nice—I feel like I have some new friends now. We have weekly meetings and it'll mean some time away from studying, but I think it's worth it. We talk about career ideas, studying for college entrance exams, financial aid for college, and how to organize your time so you can fit having fun in with homework. Next month, we're going on two trips to nearby colleges so we can see what some campuses are like. For me, being in the Honors Club has been the best part of this year.

Most of all, I feel like I belong at this school. I've found a place where I can be equal to excellence!

One of the greatest needs of any adolescent is a sense of belonging. When an adult is sensitive to adolescent development, he or she recognizes this is one of the reasons that adolescents tend to hang around in groups on street corners or push so hard to affirm ties to peers, even those a parent believes are against family-oriented values. A sense of belonging is part of the socialization process that joins an adolescent to a group and tells her, "I'm okay because they help me feel I'm okay."

Belonging to a group contributes to the development of self-image. If the group's values and goals have productive, esteeming purposes, membership in the group will go a long way toward nurturing and sustaining individual values and goals, and each member can then contribute the best of what she or he has to offer. Thus, the group is replenished as it feeds each member.

In the environment of a school, a young Black female can and does often find just such groups. In fact, the school at large forms a kind of "super-group" made up of smaller "sub-groups" with various specific purposes all contributing to the greater aims of the school. Whether the smaller groups are athletic teams, student councils, marching bands or honors clubs, each has an important role to play toward enriching and reinforcing a well-rounded education.

No one sub-group in a school has a legitimate purpose outside the educational realm, regardless of any individual tendency to overlook this reality. Athletic teams may focus so heavily on sports achievement and growing superstars that they forget the real reason young athletes are there—to obtain an education. Marching bands may get so caught up in the razzle-dazzle of their repertoire that they forget they are really learning about music as well as other subjects. And, yes, honors clubs may become attuned more to their individual scholastic standing than to their ability to contribute to the overall academic standing of their peers. So it is possible for a school's sub-groups—and hence its super-group—to forget the total, greater aim of education. But it doesn't have to happen that way, nor should it be encouraged or tolerated for it distorts the credibility of education.

In "I found my place," a young Black female discovers a school setting in which she can affirm her values and goals. Part of her discovery comes about because she has an inner understanding that she likes school, "no matter what anybody says." But "Soubretta" did not come to that recognition in a vacuum. The scenario implies that her parents had a large effect on her perspective about school. They talk to her about their values (as she mentioned during the class discussion on the civil rights movement) and she has listened to them. In addition, the environment of her former school did little to reinforce what she believed she wanted and needed from a school. Thus she has been seeking an academic setting that will complement and strengthen her and she finds just such a place.

Some may read this scenario and believe it to be an ideal school, but not a real one. For those who have not experienced a school like this, either as students or as parents of students, let me state that this story, like all the rest in this book, is based on a real situation. In fact, it was written to describe *several* such schools which I have visited over the years. Despite the unfortunate existence of schools in which the education of young people is far from being the primary objective, there are many other academic settings where exciting nurturance occurs and education of youth is examined first on an everyday basis.

I must also point out here that many of these excellent educational institutions are peopled mainly if not totally by African-Americans. This is not to say that a school cannot be excellent unless Blacks constitute its overwhelming majority. That was not my intention in having "Soubretta" feel proud that an all-Black school can achieve excellence. It would have been entirely possible, and indeed has been the case, that "Soubretta" could have experienced the same sense of belonging if she had attended an excellent school in which others such as Caucasians or Hispanics were among her teachers and fellow students. However, it does her a wealth of good to feel proud of an all-Black school that is productive, expects all its members to be equal to excellence, and provides various resources to ensure its aim.

At various points in this book, I have mentioned anomie and its four strategies. These coping mechanisms are used to seek alternative ways of adapting to a lack of institutional means for achieving cultural goals. If we look at anomie in the context of the scenario about "Soubretta," we can discover how anomie might be applied in a productive manner.

To speak of anomie in an African-American perspective is to realize that "institutional means" and "cultural goals" refer to what is or isn't provided by the dominant culture in America. In this respect, the multitude of problems in Black communities come into sharp focus: unemployment, school drop-out rates, adolescent pregnancy and infant mortality, and drug/alcohol use are among the many which come to mind. Seen from this view, a school like the one that "Soubretta" discovers is a much healthier alternative adaptation than some of the self-destructive means mentioned above. Attending a school like this provides an opportunity for a young Black female to use "rebellion" and seek to replace the dominant culture's goals with a new social structure. The school, then, becomes an institutional means for applying the "rebellion" strategy.

It could be argued that the school, since it is part of a larger institution—a system of schools—is just doing what the dominant culture usually does when it manages to succeed at providing insitutional means for achieving its cultural goals. But this statement would overlook what is just as possibly the case. The scenario does not mention this is a public school; it might also be a parochial school or a school belonging to the network known as the Council of Independent Black Institutions. When schools succeed, they do so in an organized setting—a social structure. And when schools with Black students succeed, one of the ways they do so, in a larger sense, is by replacing any goals of the dominant culture that do not reinforce or enrich values with a Black perspective, with those values and interests which do support the goals and values of African-American culture.

This is one of the primary reasons that "Soubretta" realizes her new school is a place where she can feel proud. During the discussion of the civil rights movement, she makes the critical connection between her academic values and the racial setting in which she can reinforce those values. Here we can see how an adolescent's intellectual skill of abstract thinking becomes a vital tool for her inner growth. "Soubretta," and many other Black adolescents, can value settings like schools partly because they have the level of thinking it takes to make a connection between a school and its role in their present and future lives. The teacher in the scenario must have realized this potential when he directed the discussion to have the students make connections between a social movement among Blacks and the students' individual lives. One of the greatest values of education in the lives of Black adolescents, then, is to supply a social structure in which they can be equal to excellence at precisely the time they need it and can use it most.

On a surface level, spirituality might seem to some people to be the last "place" a young Black female would go and seek help. With all the problems and issues troubling her, how is prayer going to do any good? Indeed, there are African-Americans who have abandoned Christianity, church-going, or any semblance of faith in God because they are certain God has abandoned us—why else do we face so many trials? In response to such questions (that I myself raised when I was a teenager), I will share with you the beauty and power of some moments that challenged my own view of spirituality:

The Life of the Spirit

It is Mother's Day, and I am standing in a church pew. With me is my mother, who has just finished telling me how glad she is to see me in church today. I have come mostly at her re-quest— at least that's what I've told myself. I do not feel com-fortable.

The service gets underway, and I find myself flipping through the worship book because I can't remember any of the litany passages I used to know so well as a child. Back then, going to church was strongly suggested by my parents; you could say it was forced on me, but that wasn't exactly true since I could easily have played hookey. It seemed instead to be what everybody else did, so I went.

Then a different part of the service begins. The congrega-tion is invited to submit their own prayers and speak spon-taneously. I am unaccustomed to what is for me a new part, and I find myself listening to what is being said. Middle-aged women are speaking quietly but firmly about the gratitude they feel for the mothers in their lives; some mention how much they regret not having the wisdom or courage to let their mothers know how they felt before they died. Younger voices are heard; some whisper about some awful thing they told their mothers, and how they hope that won't be held against them; others speak out in an overly loud tone as they declare their love with blanket phrases about there not being any mother in the whole universe as good as theirs.

Within me, a tiny voice reminds me of two deaths that have recently occurred: an aunt and a grandmother have both passed away in the space of a month. The voice begins to describe them to me as though it's narrating a silent movie. My mind's eye rewinds through time and I see my aunt and grandmother again—the places they took me, the way we baked bread togeth-er, the hugs we had, and the praise they freely gave me. I do not yet realize it, but I am crying as freely as the love we shared.

In a hoarse voice, I begin to tell my message to the rest of the congregation: "Lord, thank You for the women in my family. They have given me so much. But most of all, thank You for my mother—she brought me here today."

If you have ever had a spiritual experience like this one, you understand the tremendous sense of relief that prayer brings. It's as though bruising blisters lift themselves from within and are carried away. The gift of "grace" which brought that daughter to church, happened because God knew she needed to be released from her burdens. Now, with the appreciation she has gained for spirituality, it's possible that she will not only renew her relationship with a church, she will discover other avenues in which "grace" shows its presence.

"Grace," the miraculous force that is beyond our conscious will, has always served African-Americans well. I believe it is one of the "hidden strengths" to which Wade Nobles refers when he describes the forces that hold Black families together. So it is "grace" that helped "Gloria" and her mother realize the importance of a neighbor like "Mrs. Thompson," and the power of "grace" brought "Soubretta" to her new school. And it is "grace" that enables so many Black adolescents to combat sometimes tremendous odds and beat them.

The "grace" that has brought us this far, has been reinforced by faith. More than anyone else, Black people have faith in each other's capacity to use our will to shape better lives. So it remains today. There are some admirable brothers and sisters who are sacrificing high salaries, free time, large houses, and many other status symbols so they can offer our youth their greatest energies and resources. They do so out of their unshakable faith in themselves and their people.

I am aware that some who read this book do not wish to be Christians; rather, they may prefer to be Muslims, for instance. My purpose, then, is not to convince you away from your religious beliefs but to highlight the benefits a young Black female can find in drawing nearer to her spiritual self. Within this self are the keys to discovering and sustaining:

• the treasures of her culture, rooted in Africa, where women are the guardians of traditions and families know how to encourage collective and individual development;

• the resource place to go to question the hard realities of her life and find answers;

• the source that will nurture her, no matter what has happened;

• the "greenhouse" in which she can nurse her self-image and build her self-esteem.

The assumption is often made that Black adolescents aren't interested in spiritual matters; they'd rather attend to worldly affairs like popular music, clothing, and cars. Yet if the coin were flipped, it would be fair to wonder how much the churches are interested in youth. One of the reasons so many Black youth stay away from church is because they believe there isn't anything particularly geared toward them and their needs. This is not always the case; in fact, there is a growing trend within several Protestant churches to address youth absenteeism by developing programs which focus on their concerns. Of course, the degree to which churches succeed in renewing youths' faith in them will depend on whether congregations and ministers will be willing to openly confront sensitive issues like sexual intercourse, rape, adolescent pregnancy, and racism and sexism. But there is always "grace" and the gift of faith it often brings. Hopefully, Black churches will continue to strive to be one of the primary vehicles for young Black females' development. If they do, there is a variety of program needs—such as child care, child development classes, family life education, consumer education, and youth "speak-outs"—that can provide a foundation for Black adolescents to develop successful strategies for their lives.

Spirituality is like the seed at the bottom of a bag that gets tossed in the alley and forgotten for a while. But it has not forgotten itself; it has a will of its own which, with time, can emerge and flower into the source of greatly needed nourishment. So it is for a Black woman-to-be that she finds in spirituality, a source for transforming herself into a whole, proud woman. As Nannie Helen Burroughs, an outstanding Black educator, once said:

> Organize yourself inside. Teach your children the internals and eternals, rather than the externals.[12]

Self-esteem should be the main goal of any relationship.

HER FRIENDSHIPS

Relationships with Young Black Males

As they move—physically and emotionally—away from home, young Black females begin to experience the ups and downs of relating to their male peers. Naturally, they bring with them all the individual, family, community and societal "baggage" that will affect the kind of relationships they have with young males. At the same time, young brothers carry their own variety of "baggage" so there is bound to be great diversity to discover. Let's get a glimpse at some of that variety, as indicated in the following stories:

"The older the better"

Verna, age 15

Up until a year ago, I always had boyfriends my own age. But they got on my nerves 'cause I always had to put up with somethin'—either they didn't have no money, or they didn't know how to drive, so they didn't have a car. I got tired of hearin' all those excuses.

So I started goin' around with *men*, and I like that just fine. I've had maybe three or four since then. All of 'em's better than any of those *boys* I used to deal with. Me and my girlfriend Trudy we got some good men now. We met them one day when we went shopping. These two men came up to us, bold as you please, and asked us if we wanted to have lunch with them. We said sure! One of them, Slim, kept his eyes on me the whole time.

Me and Slim, we been goin' together for about two months now. Slim's 25 and he treats me real good—takes me to dinner, the movies, then we go over his place. My mama's against him 'cause she says he's takin' advantage of me bein' so much younger than him. That's not true—I mean I know I'm younger, but he gives me respect and makes me feel like a lady. Last week he brought me a pair of real nice earrings and it wasn't even my birthday. Now that's what I call a good thing!

So I say, the older the better. As far as I'm concerned, the younger ones got nothin' for me like men got to give me. I'll take a man over a boy any time 'cause a man'll take good care of you and respect you.

"My way or no way"

Sheba, age 15

People who think being a Christian is easy don't know what they're talking about. Especially when you're my age. And especially when you try to go out and have a good time. Take last Friday, for instance.

Terry asked me if I wanted to go to the basketball game after school. When I asked my parents if Terry could bring me home from the game, naturally they wanted to know more about him. I told them I didn't know him real well, but he's in two of my classes and he seems okay. So they told me it would be all right as long as we came straight to my house when the game was over.

At first, everything seemed fine. The game was exciting; one of Terry's friends made the winning basket at the last second! On the way to my house, Terry kept talking about the game so much, I could barely say a word. I didn't really mind, though; I was feelin' real good about the game too. Plus I started thinking maybe he was gonna turn out to be somebody I could go more places with. When we got to my house, my parents fixed us some sandwiches and after we ate, we played some board games for a while.

Then my father told Terry it was getting late. (That's his way of saying it's time to go.) Well, when I walked Terry out to his car, that's when the trouble started. He grabbed me and started kissin' me while one of his hands tried to squeeze my butt. I pushed him away, but he started toward me like he didn't get the message.

I told him, "Look, I don't go for that. You can't treat me like you been knowin' me a long time. You ain't my boyfriend."

His eyes got real big and he said, "What's wrong with you? Hey baby, I'm a man..."

I stopped him right there and said, "Terry, I had a good time tonight. I was startin' to think maybe we could get to know each other better. But what you just did wasn't me. I'm not for somebody kissin' me and squeezin' my body on the first time out with me. It'll take me a long time to get to that point, and I don't plan on rushin' anything. I know you think you're a man, and that's fine. I'm not tryin' to take that away from you. But I have my ways. So if we're gonna go out again, it's gonna be my way or no way."

I haven't talked to Terry since that night, and I don't know what to think of him. Maybe he'll come my way and maybe he won't. I'll still be a Christian, either way.

"Sex is not dirty"

Lisa, age 17

The best thing about me and my boyfriend is having sex. We usually do it three or four times a week—whenever we get a chance to have some privacy. Believe me, that's not easy what with his mama almost always home, and my mama watchin' me like a hawk. She says sex is wrong and I got no business messin' around. Am I blind, she's always askin' me, can't I see all of them girls walkin' around with babies and they barely out of diapers themselves?

As far as I'm concerned, can't nobody tell me sex is wrong. Feels right to me. When I'm with my boyfriend, he makes me feel so good I just want to stay with him all night. Sure, I use birth control—I'm on the pill. And yeah, a couple of times I thought I was pregnant 'cause I forgot to take it like I'm supposed to. But I try real hard to remember 'cause I ain't in this for no babies.

I'm just glad I got a man who knows what he's doin' in bed. There's been some others I thought were okay but now I wouldn't trade none of 'em for J.T. I just hope I don't get pregnant 'cause then he might run off like a lot of my friends have happen to them. I figure as long as we're makin' each other feel good, he'll come around and I'll be ready.

"He's a real friend"

Kisha, age 14

When I first met Marcus he and his family were moving into the apartment building where me and my family live. As soon as I met him, I knew he was different from the other dudes I come across. It was somethin' about the way he said hi to me—there was somethin' *real* about him.

Right away, we hit it off great. He's never lived in this city before, so since it was still summer he had some time to find his way around. I thought it was kinda strange when he asked me to show him around. I figured he'd rather do that with some dudes. I mean, he asked me like it wasn't a date or nothin' like that.

Well, I sure am glad I went—it turned out to be two weeks of some of the best times I ever had! Like I said, Marcus is different. We went places I thought you only go when you're on a class trip—to museums, the planetarium, we even went to the library. Turns out Marcus thinks those places are fun 'cause he's interested in lots of things, doesn't know what kind of job he wants, so he figures maybe he'll get some ideas from goin' places. I have to admit, I didn't know how to get to those kind of places—I wasn't spendin' much time goin' past my neighborhood. But Mama and Daddy thought it was a good idea and they helped us by writing down the directions.

Well, by the time school started, me and Marcus were fast friends. And I don't mean "fast" as in sex—no, we weren't into that. In fact, we never even held hands.

Now, I did some wondering about that at first. I mean, I didn't know if it was me, or Marcus, or what. So after about the tenth time we were out someplace, I asked Marcus, "Don't you like me?"

He looked at me funny and said, "Why would you ask that? Sure I do. Don't you like me?"

I nodded and got quiet. I was tryin' to figure out what to say and for some reason I couldn't find any words.

Then Marcus told me, "If you're wonderin' how come I'm not grabbin' on you and tryin' to move in on you, that's not my style. See, my father and I do a lot of talking. He's helped me to know some things about life. One thing I've learned—it's a whole lot better when you treat people like you want to be treated. Kisha, I like you and I want to be friends with you. But I don't want to be a boyfriend 'cause I'm not a *boy* anymore.

70

But I'm not a man yet either so I can't be your man. Matter of fact, I'm not *your* anything—I don't belong to you and you don't belong to me."

See what I mean? That Marcus—he'll put somethin' on your mind. Now that school's started, me and him won't have as much time to spend goin' places and talkin'. Marcus says he's serious about school. I don't really know what'll happen except I do know he's a real friend.

"Smack him before he hits you"

Jolene, age 14

Me and my boyfriend, we have our problems sometimes. He gets mean-headed, won't listen to me when I try to tell him somethin' he knows he should be doin'. Other times he makes me mad 'cause he says he's gonna take me to a movie or a party, and then he don't show up or he comes so late the movie's started and been over—theater's closed for hours.

Well, I don't take no mess off nobody—I don't care who you are. I'd much rather smack you upside your head than sit around and listen to some ole silly stuff. Sittin' there smilin' and sayin', "Oh that's all right. Maybe next time." Forget next time—I'll deal with it right then and let you know how my fist feels.

Mama says I'm headed straight for jail and it's just a matter of time 'til she's got to come down and get me out, regular as Tuesdays. When she says that, I just look at her hard, like what she mean, jail? Me and jail not gonna meet, not if I got somethin' to say about it.

I'm not doin' nothin' but protectin' myself. A woman's got to be strong these days 'cause somebody's always tryin' to mess with you. So when my boyfriend gets to actin' like he think he don't have to give me no respect, I smack him *before* he hits me. Then he knows not to mess with me.

"Love is wonderful, but it's hard"

Markeeta, age 16

Jimmy and me been together for six months. We met at a football game between his school and mine. Since then, we see each other every weekend and we talk on the phone almost every day. I know I'm in love and I think he feels that way too.

It hasn't been easy though. We both work on the weekends, and we're tryin' to keep our grades up so we can go to college. Seems like by the time we get through with work and studying, neither one of us has much free time. But my favorite times are when we listen to music at my house while we talk about anything and everything. After a while, we get to messin' around—you know, kissin' and huggin' and touchin' each other. But so far we've stayed away from sex 'cause Jimmy knows I'm trying to wait.

Before I met him, I spent a lot of time talking with my mother. She's been a real good mother. She's told me about everything—about menstruation, about how she had me when she was still in high school. She said she's never been sorry she had me, but she wishes she had waited 'cause she's just now going to night school for her nurse's license. And she doesn't just talk, she listens to me. We're really close.

I've told her about how I think I love Jimmy so much, it's hard not to get carried away. I feel like sex with him might be beautiful 'cause I want to experience everything with him. So I asked Mama, "When am I going to know if me and Jimmy will stay together?"

Mama listened to me and nodded. Then she said, "If lovin' him is going to be really all right, the sex part will happen when you've got *yourself* together. You ever really listen to that stuff they play on the radio? They make it sound like love and sex have to go together. But the real test is love *without* sex. If you and Jimmy can grow to love each other without havin' sex you're both going to understand more about each other than sex could ever show you. Love is much more powerful than sex—sex takes maybe 20 minutes, but love lasts a lot longer than that."

I know what Mama says is true, and Jimmy really tries to control the way he shows his affection. But it's hard—sometimes I have a tough time controlling myself.

Within these six situations are the experiences of many young Black females whose lives encounter a great variety of relationships with young Black males. The voices of "Markeeta," "Jolene," "Kisha," "Lisa," "Sheba" and "Verna" speak of love, defiance, understanding, lust, assertiveness and impatience as they—along with thousands of other sisters—face the challenge of acquainting themselves with the opposite sex.

Some, like "Sheba," are doing so with close guidance and referral from both their religious beliefs and their parents. Others, like "Jolene," are going it alone and relying on no one but themselves and their own fierce code of behavior. For those like "Kisha," whose lives are touched by someone with the courage to pursue life as the creative miracle it really can be, they come to realize that a glimpse of life's possibilities might bring a new image of male-female friendship.

Still others encounter the pleasure of physical desire and perhaps like "Lisa," they become so enamored by that pleasure, they view it as the main focus of a relationship with a male. Then again, sisters such as "Verna" don't so much wish for physical pleasure as for other things which they have come to believe they will get from older men, and which they think are signs of respect. Respect is already being shown to those like "Markeeta"; instead, she struggles with the process of balancing the romantic side of love with the longer view that is so difficult to keep in mind during adolescence.

Such is the mixture of experiences and concerns to be weighed by any female adolescent. For Black women-to-be, the mixture is flavored with an African-American perspective toward and from Black males. From this angle, in which males are developing in an arena of often competing and contradictory images and attitudes, goals like "love" and "respect" will indeed demand a combination of approaches.

Some of those approaches include the kind of toughness shown by young sisters such as "Jolene." In Chapter Two a discussion of anomie included four strategies, one of which is "innovation," in which alternative means are found for attaining cultural goals (such as a male-female relationship). When young Black females like "Jolene" treat a boyfriend with an aggressiveness that includes physical force, they are using an innovative strategy to cope with whatever difficulties or conflicts they encounter in their relationship. Jo-Ellen Asbury examined this strategy in light of males' behavior. Asbury speculated that ". . . when African-American males are unable to achieve cultural goals of masculinity through traditional means, innovation is common. These innovative strategies may include hypersexuality, concern with expressive styles of speech, dress, and appearance, *and toughness or violence*" (emphasis is mine).[1]

My view here is that African-American females, particularly the young ones, may be giving us a message of anomie. They may be telling us that, since society's treatment has been so frustrating —opening the door just a crack, then slamming it shut when it comes to real opportunities—some of them may be choosing innovative ways to cope with that frustration. It is perhaps too early for researchers to contribute to the discussion of young Black females as perpetrators of violence. But it is *not* too early for parents and other care-givers to recognize that young Black females are definitely being affected by the role violence plays in the "ball of confusion" that forms our world.

Thus, it would be wise for a Black adult in the life of someone like "Jolene" to intervene as much as possible. That is why her mother attempted to make "Jolene" see the risk she takes in behaving so aggressively. In addition, some of the other characters portrayed, such as "Lisa" who shows signs of hypersexuality, and "Verna" who focuses on older men, need intervention as well. Their mothers have tried to point out the distorted alternatives these young sisters have chosen, and perhaps their fathers can play effective roles as well. At any rate, unless these sisters choose more productive coping mechanisms, their lives and their attitudes will be unlikely to change for the better.

In terms of the kind of relationships that young Black females have with male peers, how do they define their goals? I asked the question this way in the survey I conducted: What do you think young males can do for you? The responses that follow give some clues as to what they want:

> "Support me, be a friend when I need it."
>> —a 16-year-old

> "Show me respect."
>> —a 10-year-old

> "Make me happy."
>> —a 15-year-old

> "Give me money. Have a good time [with me]."
>> —a 12-year-old

> "Nothing at all but give me a hard time."
>> —a 16-year-old

> "Help you through life."
>> —an 18-year-old

A related survey question, "When you get older, what do you expect men to do for you?" got responses like these:

> "Pay rent, gas, and light [bills] that's all."
>> —a 16-year-old

"Take care of me and my baby."

—a 16-year-old

"Nothing because if I do they is going to expect me to do something for them."

—a 13-year-old

"Buy me a car and a house."

—an 11-year-old

"Help me when I feel down. Help me raise my children."

—an 18-year-old

These responses indicate several factors that are connected to culture and gender. In light of society's historical attitude and treatment of Black males, responses such as "Nothing but give me a hard time," reflect that some of the negative attitudes toward Black males have filtered down to our young females. In addition, the more recent past, in which some tension has developed between Black men and women, is mirrored here as well. In other words, if a Black adolescent female expects nothing from Black young males or men, part of her reason for feeling that way comes from history. However, some responses do show a positive expectation; they also want, for instance, emotional support and help with family life. There is, then, a "mixed bag" of expectations.

There are other influences that contribute to the attitudes of today's Black women-to-be toward males. One of these is rooted in Black women's view that there's a shortage of Black men. What is usually meant when this comes up in conversations is that there's a shortage of *eligible and available* Black men. This is not just an issue of whether a man is unmarried; it depends also on a woman's standards regarding a man's level of formal education, income, and personality. In addition, imprisonment and participation in the military have made other Black men unavailable. The issue of unavailable Black men has its effect on Black women, and there is some awareness of this issue among their adolescent peers. The older a Black female adolescent becomes, the greater are her chances that, when she participates in activities away from home at places such as schools and churches, she may often be in settings in which few if any Black male peers are present. So the unavailability of eligible young Black males becomes more obvious to her. A subtle effect of that may be that some Black female adolescents come to focus on developing their self-sufficiency rather than relying on what the opposite sex can do for them. In those cases, any relationships they have with their male peers may seem less significant to them and not necessarily for negative reasons. They may simply be pragmatic about the situation as they see it.

Within this environment that meshes the past and present, Black and White, and family and personal circumstances, young Black females are using what is called the "model/mirror" process as they develop their relationships with young males.[2] In this process, they "model" that which is provided by concrete examples in their lives, and the amount of exposure they have to those examples affects how they model them. So, parents, adults in the neighborhood and at school, male and female peers, and images presented by the media are all potential and real models. (Even within the media there are "real" models among the fictional characters, because young people have not necessarily learned to distinguish which characters in the media are fictional.) On the other hand, the "mirror" reflects the ways in which people familiar to a youth show how they feel about her. Therefore, the "extent to which the home presents confused or negative images will affect how sensitive a kid is to values and images outside of the home."[3] Conversely, the degree to which the home presents strongly clarified or positive images will also affect a child's sensitivity to images and values outside the family nest.

In his book, *Going to the Territory*, Ralph Ellison reminds us that Black parents, as hard as they try, cannot completely combat images and values away from home; nor can they totally keep their children from adopting values or being with young peers whose behavior parents may dislike. During her adolescent years, a Black female inevitably comes into confrontation with what Ellison has called "the impact of ideas and the power of life-styles and fashion to upset custom and tradition."[4] While it's true that Black mothers and fathers have been valiant and determined in their efforts to stay together, conduct good relationships, bear children, and counteract the forces oppressing them, those forces continue to exist within the pool of ideas and images into which a young Black female swims as she negotiates her path through life.

The depth and width of that pool may be full of illusions and tricky to measure. On the one hand, it may appear to be so limited to a narrow set of lifestyles and values to which a young female will be exposed, an observer may predict that she will have a "disadvantaged" future. On the other hand, the pool may offer such a diverse series of images and ideas that when she encounters them—especially as they're filtered through the media—a certain amount of confusion and struggle are quite possible.

So it would be our mistake to make simple judgments about young Black females' relationships with male peers. They are not all engaged in destructive interactions, nor are all of them blind to the realities that exist within the males they pursue. In addition, they have not necessarily "given up" on Black males if they say they expect "nothing" from them. If we adults limit ourselves to any of these predictions, we not only devalue the strengths of our culture, we overlook whatever qualities Black adolescents have within themselves to bring to the table of their relationships.

So responses like, "buy me a car and a house," imply that, yes, adults ought to be concerned about hearing a desire for a relationship in which dependency and material support are the primary motives. On the other hand, some of that desire is rooted in two influences: they're still young and still want some degree of support which they view more or less in tangible terms; these tangibles are also responses to the dominant culture's materialism—a "buy, buy, buy and more, more, more" attitude that connects purchasing power with adulthood and the "good life."

And when a Black female adolescent expects a male peer to get her pregnant, certainly our concern should increase greatly, because we know that early pregnancy will cause her to join a cycle of challenges for which she's largely unprepared. Getting out of that cycle will take education, employment, consistent and affordable child care, and knowing about child development so she can rear a healthy offspring. At the same time, we need to focus on the flip side: she might see pregnancy as an everyday fact of life around her home or community and as such, she may be noticing the predictability for herself given the odds. (This is not to say we should not try to persuade her that she could beat the odds.) In addition, if there's enough of an absence of male-female relationships in which sexual intercourse or reproduction is clearly not the focus, she may understandably have trouble imagining them. And if she has no concrete reasons for delaying pregnancy, adults can lecture her tirelessly and she can be fully aware of methods of birth control, but she may not use the information in the actions she takes.

Responses like, "show me respect" should get our attention and admiration, because they indicate a desire to be treated fairly and positively by the opposite sex. We also ought to treat those responses as part of a young Black female's concrete reality and not as some childish daydream. From her point of view, expectations like these are not fairy tales—they are real demands she intends to achieve.

In the meantime, young Blacks attempt to have relationships with each other. Thus, they are doing and learning at the same time, and this twofold process—to effectively enhance future relationships—needs self-esteem as the primary goal.

The different ways in which "Verna," "Jolene," "Kisha," "Sheba," "Lisa" and "Markeeta" treat their male peers is affected greatly by whether they are actively striving for self-esteem and whether they understand what they must do to achieve a love of self. So when someone like "Jolene" believes she must use physical violence or its threat to relate to males, she uses the coping strategy of "innovation" as an alternative to achieving a self-esteeming relationship with her boyfriend. And when a young Black female like "Sheba" declares that her relationships with young males will go "her way or no way," she too seeks an "innovative" strategy but she does it according to self-esteeming values. Christine Carrington explains the importance of self-esteem when she states: "Self-hate has to be replaced by self-love, indignity with dignity, depriving love objects with nurturing love objects, feelings of victimization with feelings of power and mastery."[5]

When it comes to young Black females, two concerns seem to be most commonly shared. They want to have relationships with Black males, but they are increasingly insisting that those relationships happen on their terms—even when their standards are still being developed or seem to contradict long-term needs. In the next section, some sisters share how they help each other pinpoint and reinforce standards of behavior.

A Sisterhood Among the Young

Sisters see other Black women as family, not as competition for men. They know that belittling someone doesn't attract boyfriends. It only loses girlfriends. Sisters understand each other like no one else can. They need each other. Sisters survive through each other, because when the world keeps knocking them down they have each other to fall back on.[6]

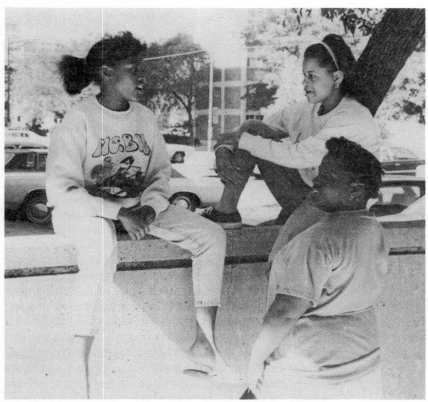

Sisters understand each other like no one else can.

As hard as the media and other societal forces try to make sisterhood into a lie or a fantasy, its reality is firmly locked into African-American culture and history. Long before it became fashionable during the 1960s and 1970s for Black women to call each other "Sister," their church-going forebears could be heard identifying each other the same way. And centuries before any of us arrived on these shores with the prospect of enforced inhumanity, family life in West Africa—for example among the Ashanti people—was preserved and reinforced by Black women such as the *Ohemaa* (queen mother). She was usually the king's mother or sister, and as such she served as the official genealogist, supervisor of female initiation ceremonies into womanhood, and the senior female of the Ashanti.[7] As such, the Ohemaa's position made her a symbolic as well as a practical leader of her people and a strong role model for all other Ashanti women. And since she guided the female initiations into womanhood, she served as the leading force of Ashanti sisterhood.

In what ways do Black females preserve the traditions and attitudes of centuries ago? How do young Black females show they are each other's sisters? Is sisterhood among young Black females an ideal or a practical reality? Perhaps if we listen in on some of the conversations among young sisters, we will learn some answers to those questions. What follows is a series of roundtable discussions of various young sisters' viewpoints about situations and attitudes they encounter from each other and those around them.

Has motherhood been like you thought it would be?

Jeannette: I figured my baby would be just like anybody else's child already in my family. I got 8 brothers and sisters, and half of 'em are younger than me, so I'm used to kids. It's pretty much the same now. Feedin' him, checkin' on him while he sleeps, havin' to be home a lot—I did that before.

Mae: Not me. I'm the youngest so I always had somebody around to take care of *me*, not the other way around. It's hard to get used to always havin' to be ready to do somethin' for my daughter. Seems like she wants somethin' every two minutes. When she gonna need me less, that's what I want to know.

Jeannette: How old is she?

Mae: Three weeks come tomorrow.

Cynthia: Oh, she'll get better about that in a few more weeks, around when she's maybe three or four months, she'll sleep longer periods. Thing is, babies keep changin'. Soon they get to bein' awake longer, then you really got a job on your hands. My son, he's two, and let me tell you... *(she shakes her head)*

Karen: "Terrible two's"—mine's goin' through that too. I can't turn my head on that child for two seconds. I can be busy in the kitchen or watchin' my soaps and quick as a flash—she's off somewhere and into somethin' or other. She

	keeps me hoppin'. Sometimes I just want to scream 'cause I can't get a minute's rest from her.
Jackie:	Yeah, rest—what's that? Ain't had no rest the last three years, ever since Darryl was born. *(They all nod.)*
Debra:	The thing that gets to me is when I take my baby to do some shoppin'. I'm wheeling him around and tryin' to pick him out some clothes, and meanwhile my daughter—she's two—she's all the time tuggin' on me and grabbin' anything she can get her hands on, and Petey gets to cryin' 'cause he's hungry or wet or whatever. And just when I've just about had it and I'm either gonna cry or yell or just haul everybody home—forget about shoppin' just let me sit down in peace—know what always seem to happen?
Jeannette:	Girl, what?
Debra:	Somebody, almost always some woman—she sees me in all this mess I'm tryin' to deal with and she gives me this *look* like I'm some kinda trash shoulda crawled into a hole and stayed there. Like ain't I doin' the best I can, can't she see that? And do you think she offers to help me? Or at least stop lookin' at me like that—now that really kills me. I get so mad I don't know which is worse, the kids or her.
Jeannette:	Really. That's the truth.
Maisha:	I just wish I had known I was gonna get interested in drawin' designs for decoratin' homes *before* I got pregnant. Ever since I showed some of my pictures to a lady who came to the social center, I been squeezin' every minute I can to work on this decoratin' thing. Soon as my husband comes home from night class, I get up and work on my designs.
Mae:	Where you get money from to decorate your place? Your husband must be treatin' you good.
Maisha:	I'm not workin' on my place, I'm tryin' to make designs for *any* place. That lady down to the social center said she thought my designs were good, and I should keep workin' on 'em. Maybe

I could get me a job or get in a school. Don't get me wrong—me and my husband get along fine, I probably would've married him, baby or no baby. But if I hadn't had our baby so soon, maybe I could be workin' right now.

The comments of these adolescent mothers sound strikingly similar to those among adult women. Here again, the maturity level discussed in Chapter Two is present among the adolescents in this roundtable. In their day-to-day lives, all of them are taking on responsibilities—like child care, shopping, and career development—which might be postponed among their Caucasian peers for many years. In addition, they express some varied reflections on the state of their lives as mothers. One mentions regret because her newfound career choice will be more difficult to reach; another is angry about the way outsiders view her, while still another adolescent mother is resigned to motherhood—it doesn't seem different to her than the child rearing she did for her brothers and sisters. What is important to notice as well are the ways in which these sister/mothers try to help each other. One provides advice about early childhood, so the other will understand her baby's behavior. Another adolescent mother affirms her sister's frustration with the world by agreeing that her viewpoint is understandable.

Throughout, there's a certain wistfulness about their lives as young mothers. Many of them have realized—through actual experience—that life as a mother has been quite different from their expectations. Some of them wish they might have somehow been able to understand its demands before they experienced them.

What's the "real deal" with Black men—where do they stand in your lives and you in theirs?

Linda:	Can't live with 'em and can't live without 'em —that's what I say. Take my boyfriend...
Aretha:	Fine by me. I could use another one! *(laughs)*
Linda:	I mean it. He's got too many moods for me to live with. One day he's as sweet as he can be, next day, you better walk on water or he's upset in a minute. Smallest thing and he just goes off.

	I couldn't deal with all those changes if we was under the same roof. I got too many other things to do besides pay attention to him all the time.
Rita:	What else you got?
Linda:	Hey, I got track practice, school, parties . . . He ain't the be-all, end-all. Why should he be? He don't pay my bills and don't pay Mama's neither.
Rita:	I heard that! Some of these men, they think they run your life 24 hours a day. Be different if they had a *reason* to act that way.
Aretha:	Reason or not, none of 'em got exclusive rights on me, I don't care what they say. They can sweet-talk me all they want . . .
Linda:	Oooh, and can't they talk sweet?! It's like they stand in front of a mirror and practice sayin' just the right words, then they check to see if they face got just the right look when they say it.
Aretha:	Naw, here's what they do. They sit around and practice so they can help each other out. One of 'em will say: "Baby, you know I just *got* to be with you, like, all the time you got, I want. I mean, I'm for real, you know?" *(everyone laughs loudly)*
Rita:	Girl, you know it must be that way. 'Cause they be sayin' the same ole stuff, over and over and over . . .
Linda:	S.O.S. You got it.
Aretha:	That's why I just take their stuff like my mama say—"go with the flow." 'Cept I do like *some* of that flow.
Linda:	Girl, how you sound? *(laughs)*
Rita:	She's tellin' it like it is. They got some flow, some of 'em got some moves can move *you*.
Aretha:	Pretty moves, all right. Now if we could just get 'em to have the babies *and* pay the bills . . .
Linda:	Be all right then. 100% all right. *(everyone smiles and nods)*

This conversation, between three Black females in their late adolescent years, displays some frank views. A "no-holds-barred" approach is used as it often is among Black females, no matter what their age. As they speak openly, they confront and accept each other's behavior and opinions about sexual intercourse, males, and the flaws and contradictions they encounter. Humor is used too; it helps them cope with their frustrations as they try to counteract deception, game-playing, and the unpredictability that comes with any male-female relationship.

There are no babes in the woods among these sisters. They may be only 17, but they're sophisticated in their awareness of their physical needs, communication patterns, boyfriends' moods and other facets of male-female relations that their older peers are still examining. They may be aware, but they are still struggling to resolve some stumbling blocks. The difficulty of seeking self-fulfillment has made them knowledgeable about the treatment they're getting from males, but they're still held back from self-esteeming relationships, partly because of the coping strategies they use.

For example, one of the ways that "Rita" deals with young Black males is with the strategy of "innovation." She feels that, although she isn't pleased with their game-playing, the alternative of hypersexuality—concentrating on sexual intercourse as the emphasis of a relationship—makes her contact with males acceptable. "Aretha" has found that she copes best by using "ritualism," which allows her to tolerate her dealings with young Black males because she has lowered her expectations of them. By trying to concentrate her time on activities like track practice, school and parties, "Linda" uses "rebellion" to try and replace an emphasis of a male-female relationship with other socializing tools.

As each tries to help the other deal with the conflict and tension they experience in their relationships, a great deal of effort will be needed to foster self-love beyond the realm of sexual intercourse. Not to do so might bring these sisters a cycle of despair. The same situations peopled by males with the same characteristics, will be repeatedly treated with the same, inadequate, self-defeating attitudes and methods. The result will be a familiar feeling of failure and frustration. No amount of humor can really substitute for success in a male-female relationship. At the same time, with greater self-esteem, these sisters will begin to see new options to their current attitude of accepting any unproductive behavior they find in themselves and their men. Unless awareness brings with it a new viewpoint armed with different approaches, time passes like suspended animation and growth is just a way of marking off birthdays on a calendar.

Are Black girl gangs on the rise and if so, why do you think that is happening?

Tree:	Well, we don't like to call 'em "gangs" but we got some "social clubs" gettin' they names known on the street. Course, some been around a long time with the men. You know, they hook up with they brothers and stay with 'em, all the way live.
Tamara:	Yeah, one of my sisters, she joined up long time ago. She too old now and got her kids to take care of but she still say, "I'm a 'Black Disciple Queen'—they made me, and they never let me down."
Tree:	Well, I don't know about them Black Disciples, I'm a "Troop Leader" myself. Me and a bunch of my friends got together two months ago, and we took a vote and named ourselves Troop Leaders. We up to 30 members now.
Sweet Pea:	What you all do when you meet?
Tree:	Bunch of stuff, go skatin' on Thursdays, trip out [hang around their neighborhood] on Fridays, have our meetins' on Saturdays, then sometimes Saturday nights get real live...
Tamara:	Get down to it?
Tree:	Yeah, buddy, we get to talkin' in our meetins' about some b_ _ _ _ from over the border [territorial "line" separating gangs] who took it into her crazy head to mess with one of my Troops. Or somebody's baby sister calls up and tells us she scared to come home 'cause she went to a movie and didn't know there'd be a bunch of "Diamond Ladies" sittin' in the movie. So all the Troops go stormin', we march tough, we don't play when it's our time to go!
Sweet Pea:	Don't sound like no fun to me.
Tamara:	Aw "P," you too young to know about that. Next year, you'll see. Tree tryin' to tell you.

	When it's your time to go, you'll be glad you got somebody to back you up. That's why I respect my ladies. They'll make you . . .
Tree:	*(interrupts Tamara)* Yeah, or break you if you get in our way. *(pulls a carpet knife out of her jacket pocket)* I don't think twice about usin' this if I see I got to protect my Troops and they own. No time for thinkin', got to be ready to act when things get live. *(puts the knife back in her pocket)* 'Til then, we cool—we out to have some fun. But mess with us, well, we together—just like this. *(makes a tight fist)*

Gang involvement by young Black females occurs in the context of society's view of violence in general and violence toward and by females. In an area of popular culture that is more directly related to females, a discussion of violence in America would be incomplete without bringing up some of the movies being produced and featured in theatres around the country. In particular, one type comes to mind: those in the "gory" vein (no pun intended) in which there is always a young female being brutally attacked by a monstrous, sometimes supernatural creature. At first, this kind of movie may have seemed like just a weak fad that would die out after a few versions made their appearances in theaters. But over a period of about eight years, from 1980 to 1988, movies of this sort have not gone away; instead, we've been treated to either seemingly endless sequels (they're up to Part 13 in some cases), or repeated plots in which only the names have changed. A closer examination, then, is worthwhile to understand their impact.

On an obvious level, movies in which the female character is brutally stabbed, beaten, electrocuted, set afire, and otherwise bludgeoned beyond recognition cannot possibly serve any positive purpose for viewers, particularly young ones. Beyond that level, though, there is additional damage done. By being shown at reputable theaters and given large advertising space and time in the media, not only is violence given an acceptable appearance, in these movies, violence is used as a *stimulator*—it excites audiences in much the way that Frankenstein, the werewolf, and other monsters of the cinema used to excite movie-goers during the 1950s. The trouble is, when shocking, brutal acts fill two hours on the screen, the next such "blood-'n'-gore" film will need even more shock value if it's going to pack the house. Viewers, then, tend to get numbed by graphic violence and movie directors have to come up with another, bigger blast. And another, and another, and another—until one wonders how much gorier they can possibly get.

Of course, the other question concerns why directors choose *females* to be the victims. Could it be that females are seen as helpless, or that they supposedly deserve this kind of treatment? I raise these questions not to engage in a lot of psychological discussion that might, in the end, be fruitless, but to lift the curtain over gory movies so they begin to be considered as a large part of what influences Black adolescent females. As such, the movies add brutality to the dominant culture's devalued attitude toward young females.

The flip side of this argument is that one of the most popular series of films of this type features a female character who was attacked in the previous movies, but who has now become the attacker. She's the one who is now bludgeoning, electrocuting, setting afire, etc. Is turnabout fair play here? From the long lines to buy tickets and the high interest measured in the faces and reactions of audiences—many of whom are Black female preteens and teens—one would guess that fans of these movies think it's not only fair, it's fine with them. In addition, their presence at these theaters, as well as the absence of fullscale protests on the part of adults against the showing of these films, tells adolescents that in effect the movies are okay to see. So the toleration level for violence, it seems, has expanded to include violent acts committed by females themselves. Black female gangs are partly shaped by popular movies that feature violence, and this factor should not be overlooked.

Gang names like "Black Disciple Queen," "Diamond Ladies," and "Troop Leaders" manipulate language and meaning into what is shaped by their lives' conditioning. Like the male gangs that began their rise years ago, "Black" in this sense puts a self-hating twist to the pride and self-worth intended by Blackness. In addition, by calling themselves "Disciple Queens," the image emerges of followers of a royal lineage—if only they focused on self-love rather than self-destruction. "Diamond Ladies" also brings the illusion of worth as well as femininity—interestingly, femaleness is matched here with the cold, hard gleam of a gem that can cut glass. The name mentioned by "Tree"—"Troop Leaders"—

originates in a popular brand of clothing that has come to be a status symbol among Black youth. On another level, "Troop Leader" is also connected to a military image that's reinforced by being in charge.

Female gang members have imitated their male counterparts in other language they use. Phrases like, "all the way live," "your time to go," and "make you or break you" make it clear that violence has its place among the so-called "social clubs" they have formed. Conflicts, and their resolution by physical force, stamp a mark as true as the "borders" surrounding their territories. People like "Tamara," who says she gives her respect to her "ladies" (the peers she knows are gang members), are viewed as few and far between in the eyes of these gang members. Probably some hard-earned lessons as well as the neighborhood grapevine have taught them a vigilante style of justice. As so often happens when people engage in violence to solve problems, violence has seduced "Tree" and others like her. It has seemed not only acceptable, but attractive—and once she's pulled into its power, she has come to believe in its effectiveness as the way "to go" to be "live." "All the way live," then, means more than a wholehearted involvement in violence. It is also a commitment given from which will come a distorted sense of being alive and secure within the support of a group similarly bound by brutality.

It should be pointed out that "Tree" is the only one of the three who admits to gang membership. "Sweet Pea" appears to be curious about gang activity but seems displeased and perhaps scared by the descriptions of Saturday night activities. "Tamara," who is older than "P," has apparently been shrewd about gangs. She's pragmatic about their existence, and having known about them from her sister's participation, she accepts them. On the other hand, "Tamara" never implies that she intends to join a gang. Instead, she gives them her "respect," probably in whatever way it's demanded of her. Her tolerance of gangs, as wily as it seems, seduces "Tamara" too. Caught in the web of the interwoven relationships between gang members and non-gang members, she does not hesitate to tell "Sweet Pea" that she will develop the same acceptance in exchange for protection. "Tamara" represents anyone in a community who believes she can do nothing to stop gangs.

To be sure, protection—whether believed or actual—must seem inadequate to these and other young Black females forming gangs today. They often live in areas with either insufficient police officers, calls with a slow response time, or an attitude toward American law enforcement that is deeply embedded in bitterness and distrust. So Black adults become a key factor. If their alert contact with Black female youth is consistent, there will be signals of a perceived or actual need among them for greater protection from crime. Consistent contact will also reinforce a support network to which Black girls can go and seek help if they think it will be provided whenever they need it. And if such a network maintains its association, Black women-to-be can use it as a vehicle to form different clubs than the one "Tree" has joined.

It is reasonable to guess that anomie exists among Black youth who form or join gangs. Since 1973, the Children's Defense Fund, a national fact-gathering and lobbying group, has been publicizing the inequitable, shameful treatment by society of children, especially Black children. In her book, *Families in Peril*, Marian Wright Edelman, the president of CDF, notes:

> Compared to white children, we found that black children are
> *twice as likely to . . .*
> • see a parent die
> • live in substandard housing. . .
> • be unemployed as teenagers
> • have no parent employed. . .
> *three times as likely to*
> • be poor...
> • be in foster care
> • die of known child abuse;
> . . .*five times as likely to*
> • be dependent on welfare; and
> • *twelve times as likely to*
> • live with a parent who never married.[8]

Seen in this light, there is little wonder why Black female youth might feel a growing sense of anomie, and react with one of the four coping mechanisms (innovation, ritualism, retreatism, and rebellion). Of these strategies, only rebellion provides a constructive means for long-term change among the greatest number of people. But rebellion needs a positive social structure; otherwise, it takes on forms such as gang organization and a youth who might certainly be and become an activist for herself and her people, instead becomes a loser.

The young Black females in your community may not be forming gangs. Yet there is another point that emerges from the gang roundtable which applies to any community in which Black women-to-be and their families live. During this stage in their development, they are struggling to deal with social growth. Peer-to-peer contact and involvement in group activities are the general ways in which they handle social growth. More specifically, though, adolescent social development represents an opportunity for adults to direct that development in meaningful, productive ways. Black female gang involvement is more than disruptive behavior among a group of "bad" girls. It is an attempt—however destructive—by young sisters to deal with an absence of productive group settings that will contribute to their present and future lives. So by including the gang roundtable here, I hope to stimulate your interest in making sure there are many opportunities for social growth among the young Black females in your community.

In your home, does music ever cause arguments? Why or why not?

Shantel: Everybody at my house listens to the same songs. The only time we argue about music is when somebody wants to play the stereo and other people want to watch TV. But other than that, we all like the same music.

Carol: Not with my family. Grandmama's always complainin' about the tapes we play and the videos we watch. She says she wishes we'd listen to church music 'cause she thinks the music we like is the devil's work. Mama's not as old-fashioned but she can't get into house music or rap, and that's what me and my sisters like the best. So most of the time we have to wait until they're not home or else use our headphones, which is hard—we ain't got but two pair between the four of us.

Tracy: We used to argue about music until a year ago, when I joined the school band. Daddy and Mama always yelled at me about the songs on the radio—they kept sayin' there wasn't anything worth hearin' because of what they said

	was "the junk in those songs."
Carol:	Don't they always say that?
Tracy:	Sure did, especially when I told 'em what I really wanted to do was play music. Then they went off like the Fourth of July!
Shantel:	What happened then? How'd you get 'em to let you play music?
Tracy:	Well, you know if you really want somethin', you got to keep at it. And they could tell how bad I wanted to play 'cause no matter how much they yelled, I always found a way to keep listenin'. So finally we had a long talk. They agreed to let me learn how to play music and I agreed to really work at it. That's when I joined the band.
Carol:	You never played before?
Tracy:	Sure didn't.
Carol:	Then how'd you get in the band?
Tracy:	Well, it took a lot of beggin' but lucky for me, the band is new so Mr. Garrett, the band teacher, he was willing to let me try. I told him I'd practice all night and every night if he just give me a chance on a saxophone—that's what I've had my mind set on. And ever since then, I been blowin' like crazy. *(she laughs loudly)*
Shantel:	A saxophone? I never heard of no woman playin' a saxophone. Where'd you get the idea to play that?
Tracy:	Don't know exactly. I guess the saxophone's always been what I like to hear and I can't see why I can't play one. Anyway, now that I've been in the band, we don't argue about music anymore. And with all the practicin' I have to do, the few times I listen to the radio now, I hear things differently.
Carol:	What you mean by that?
Tracy:	It's like I hear songs on the radio for the way they're put together. I hear 'em better than I heard 'em before. I can pick out some of the notes and I got a better idea of how to play 'em. Some of the songs I thought were good before, don't sound so good now. And you know, somethin' else has happened.
Shantel:	What?

91

Tracy:	The other day, Daddy surprised me. He bought me a tape to hear. Said it was somebody I might want to listen to now that I'm serious about playin'. So I played the tape and you know, this dude can really jam!
Shantel:	Who is he?
Tracy:	His name's John Coltrane.
Carol:	John who? Never heard of him. Is he somebody new?
Tracy:	He's new to me, but Daddy said he been dead a long time. Dead or alive, that man sure can blow a sax! I get excited every time I listen to him 'cause he makes me want to just keep on practicin'. If I can play even half as good as he did, I just might make it with my music.
Carol:	Wouldn't that be somethin'? We could be talkin' to a future saxophone star—Miss Tracy Wilson! *(they all laugh)*

As they discuss the role that music plays in family disagreements or harmony, "Shantel," "Carol" and "Tracy" reveal some interesting issues. Each of them makes it clear that their parents' views about music affect them; "Shantel" says there is no disagreement, so her and her parents' musical tastes must be closely similar. "Carol" points to two differences among the adults in her household: her grandmother heavily favors gospel music, while her mother prefers that "Carol" and her sisters play something other than house or rap music. As for "Tracy," the disagreement she experiences tends more toward the content ("there wasn't anything worth hearin' because of the junk in those songs") than the style of the songs she and her parents argued about. In this roundtable, then, there is a diversity of opinions about music from younger and older alike, and it is clear that the three young sisters' parents and other adult care-givers are actively involved in developing the girls' musical interests.

What does this roundtable have to do with a sisterhood among our young? When the discussion is viewed through the perspective of African-American women and their attitude toward each other, the quotation about sisters at the beginning of this section comes to mind. The three young Black females in the roundtable don't belittle each other; when "Tracy" tells the others about her aspiration to become a saxophonist, "Shantel" responds with curiosity—she admits her ignorance, but she doesn't insult "Tracy" for wanting to play the saxophone. In addition, "Carol" and "Shantel" support "Tracy" for her ability to go beyond being a listener to becoming a musician. They respond favorably to her statements and they indicate they can be depended upon to continue their support if she "makes it with her music" and becomes a professional.

There is one other element of sisterhood in this roundtable. It is more subtle, yet it is demonstrated nonetheless. Sisters have always contributed to the reinforcement of cultural values such as understanding and support; in addition, they have contributed to the preservation of artistic traditions and values. I purposely included this roundtable to highlight some of the ways in which a young Black sisterhood can and does contribute to the keeping and reinforcing of artistic traditions and beliefs. Appreciating and gaining skill in music, dance, jewelry and other arts is not the sole territory of Black females. However, I believe this is an area of life in which our young sisters already show some tangible interest (especially in popular music and dance, for instance), and it can be an avenue for promoting less tangible growth in attitudes and treatment of each other. In short, a sisterhood among our young people can be fertile ground for planting seeds that reinforce self-esteem. By encouraging and supporting each other's interests and aspirations, young Black females build a network of ties to "fall back on" whenever they need the nurturing sense of family that sisterhood provides.

This is the essence of sisterhood, as hinted in the various roundtables you read. When it is actively developed, a young sisterhood can join with a young brotherhood to total a strong community of Black youth. And that can someday come to mean a strong community of Black people.

Stream of thought: boys & girls, men & women

all I want is for a man to appreciate me as much as I want
    to appreciate myself:
don't want to be shortchanged
want to enjoy a person's company just for what it is
& not for what it's supposed to be or could be later
    (in bed?)
don't want to be taken care of

want to share,
don't want to feel like I'm taking care of someone
(an invalid must feel awfully vulnerable)
want to express my needs, wishes, even vulnerable moods
without feeling like I've given away parts I'll never get back
in kind,
can't open myself up without that kind of openness shown;
is that so bad?
sometimes I wish I could tell boys & girls about this
period of life;
feel as though many peers (single women) waste so much
valuable time.[9]

APPROACHING CHANGE

The development of Black female adolescents is complex and the process of their growth involves multiple layers affected by several factors. Therefore, if adults are to contribute meaningfully to that process, certain issues need to be addressed. One of those issues involves how we adults have managed in this area in the recent past.

The question might seem an obvious one, since it's easy to state that we have simply failed; therefore, whatever approach was used, it was not the right one. That view itself is inadequate. We have not so much failed as we have tended to use partial or simplistic methods. Some examples of inadequate approaches include:

• identifying a group too narrowly (as in only using older adolescents);

• identifying needs too narrowly (this has happened when a program only focuses on adolescent females' sports activity without informing them of related concerns such as dietary needs, health care, etc.);

• approaching needs simplistically (this kind of program might view adolescent Black females as having only one area of interest like dancing; another simplistic error has been the kind of program that glosses over details that make or break a program like its location in terms of gang territories, or not conducting sufficient background, which causes simplistic conclusions to be drawn if participants' attendance falls off).

In the interest of fairness, it should be stated that many programs serving Black female adolescents have succeeded in one area or another. In addition, rarely have there been public sector funds available for program development to thrive with public support. There are indications that renewed support will perhaps come from the federal government, but as any program administrator knows, public funds can dry up—sometimes when a program is just beginning to take effect.

That brings me to another failure adults have made in their involvement with Black female adolescents. There has been a tendency to work with this developmental process as though it will be over in two or three years. As was pointed out in Chapter One, areas of growth—particularly in terms of the social, intellectual, and emotional aspects—need time to develop. It is physical growth which tends to be limited in time. Thus it would be reasonable to wonder whether, in approaching Black female adolescence in this limited manner, some adults are falling prey to myth-making. In other words, by assuming an adolescent female's physical growth spurt is about all there is to deal with, has that had a subtle influence on the duration of a program's involvement with her? I raise this question to make you aware of the need to address all her areas of development to make a maximal contribution to her future.

The topic of myth-making reminds me of a related reaction from some adults. When it comes to Black female adolescents (as well as young Black males), a perception exists among some adults that these segments of our society aren't "worth" additional effort or time spent. This is when racist and sexist myths ingrain themselves in attitudes and behavior, because it is easy to forget that Black youth are our tomorrow—it is not so much true that we inherited our culture, but that we are *borrowing it from our youth*. If we turn our backs on them, we will have given up on the future of us as a culture. They don't need less attention, they need more.

By denying our responsibility for their lives, we endanger our short- and long-term futures. An educator once mentioned to me that he's afraid we may have already lost the bulk of the present adolescent population. He pointed to the increasing "dropping out" by young Black males from structured, productive settings like school, and the increasing "falling in" by them to self-destructive settings like prison, homeless shelters, and just plain old street corners. The limitations placed on young Black females in terms of available males with goals and lifestyles in common with theirs has a great chance of continuing if not increasing into their futures as adults. Thus the cycle of singlehood, female-headed households, and males absent from the process of family life would repeat itself until—three or four generations from now—Black males will have put themselves (and us) out of existence.

A thoroughly pessimistic view? Not completely; the *possibility* exists because we have not broken the cycle yet. But we have opportunities to do so at present, and those of us with the skills, resources, and time ought to get serious about their need for us.

What may cause some hesitation is the tremendous level of needs. From the viewpoint of one whose involvement has previously been minimal at best, the picture might appear hopeless or at least indicative of a vacuum cleaner, sucking up all you have to give. At this point I'd like to inject some hopefulness, based on what I believe to be a substantive alternative.

In my view, the bottom line of all these inadequacies regarding Black female adolescent development is that a fundamental change in approach is needed. If you have ever met any Black females who are young adults (and thus recently emerged from adolescence), it becomes clear fairly fast whether they have passed through adolescence with any meaningful effectiveness. If they have, these young people often have goals they are working hard to achieve; they use a variety of resources to make progress in their lives; they maintain values which are consistent with their goals; they use their time well and in varied ways. They are determined young adults who have managed their way through adolescence with a great deal of success.

Why? What caused them to develop effectively? I think it would be reasonable to guess that they approached their adolescent years—or at least some of those years—by using a fundamentally different approach than those of so many of their peers. The description I gave of effective Black young adults included areas of social, emotional, and intellectual growth. By approaching these areas in a substantially different manner, a young person has a much greater chance of entering young adulthood with an increased level of self-esteem.

Beyond individual success stories, a fundamentally different approach toward young Black females has a greater chance of effectiveness with a wider group of people. There is also a greater chance of long-term effect, so when they reach adulthood, they are carrying with them some tools to draw upon and reinforce throughout their lives.

This kind of approach allows for a balance between problems and weaknesses and solutions and strengths. Instead of continuing the ongoing trend—especially among dominant culture myth-makers—of concentrating solely on negative behavior among our youth, an approach that's essentially different uses the forces that created those behaviors as the starting point for changing them. For instance, with this kind of approach, young Black females who are interested in group activity—but have begun forming gangs—can be redirected to become a group of peer advisors who offer support and encouraging techniques to potential gang members in their community. Likewise, those who have become adolescent mothers with limited incomes, a G.E.D. and a desire to work, can be among the people who work at a child care center, where they can lend their knowledge about child rearing. These are but two of the multitude of ways we can turn problems into solutions for more than one individual.

In addition, an approach that is fundamentally different must take into account the need for social change that will benefit the present and future existences of our young females. For far too long, too many methods have overlooked the issue of community development when it comes to adolescent growth. They do not exist solely in their homes or at their schools. They live in communities which can contribute to strengths and solutions, and which can be enhanced by productive, substantive adolescent involvement. Thus an example of how this new approach might be effective would be in targeting facilities for adolescent programs, forming a community-wide coalition of groups and other interested residents whose sole purpose is adolescent development, and working with community businesses to expand their involvement with adolescents through jobs, fund-raising sponsorships, and college scholarships. There are some communities where these kinds of ideas are already in effect, and where they exist, improvement has already been noticed in the lifestyles and attitudes of Black adolescents involved.

Perhaps the greatest difficulty when it comes to fundamental change is within ourselves. Adolescents have a way of making you confront yourself in terms of your attitudes and behavior toward them, as well as the kind of role model you provide for them. Thus your involvement with adolescent Black females becomes a two-way process in which communication of values and attitudes makes or breaks the effectiveness of the relationship. Our involvement, then, is our opportunity to improve our own self-esteem and the way in which we exhibit self-worth.

At the root of a fundamental change is a cultural approach. By linking individual growth to a cultural approach, it will mean drawing adolescent Black females closer to all that we as African-Americans believe and do. It will require affirming ourselves as a people with distinctive outlooks, traditions, and coping mechanisms. A cultural approach will make our young people more familiar with an element of themselves that has enabled all our past generations to survive. Finally, a cultural approach will empower them to face the future with a better preparation than many of them now receive.

Essentially, I am speaking of recreating our culture. For one of the sad realities I have come to learn about today's Black adolescents is that a great many of them have inadequate knowledge about their culture. Yes, some of them know a few Black heroes and heroines of the past, and many of them know about Black celebrities in sports and entertainment. Yet they frequently have little if any in-depth knowledge about processes of development, instigating influences of protest and change, and the role that Africa has played on an internal level.

It is in these areas that young Blacks need cultural renewal, and Black adolescent females may provide a key to reinforcing the change among the rest of us. They are the present and future mothers who will have a great effect as role models and enculturating forces for their children. If a cultural change occurs within them, the culture will have agents to pass along their knowledge to future generations. As Maulana Karenga noted:

> The solution to the black family and community crisis begins and progresses within the context of cultural struggle . . . Without such a total approach, all efforts will eventually prove inadequate.[1]

The writer of those words conceived a set of principles which find application in the area of cultural change. The next chapter will explore how these principles have been activated, and who among us has, perhaps unknowingly, made the principles of cultural growth a day-to-day part of their lives.

School can strengthen nia (purpose) and imani (faith).

NURTURING HER FUTURE: PRACTICAL POSSIBILITIES

One of the primary purposes of this book is to give life to ideas and situations that will enrich your thinking and behavior toward young Black females. In doing that, it became clear to me that you would then need a set of starting points to collect what you have discovered here—as well as in your own experiences—into a cohesive whole. With a body of starting points, you would have a frame to refer to, and a direction to guide you. The Nguzo Saba represent an effective frame of reference to use.

Also known as the "Seven Principles of Blackness," the Nguzo Saba began in 1966 and have usually been associated with the holiday Kwanzaa.[1]

However, it has occurred to me that they apply on a more comprehensive level than one holiday. In fact, I am sure that they are meant to be implemented on an everyday basis. When I began viewing the Nguzo Saba in that manner, I noticed their implementation in the past and present. Thus, the creator of the Nguzo Saba, Dr. Maulana Karenga, has verbalized a philosophy that is already there. These starting points have been used throughout our historic struggle to empower ourselves individually and collectively.

The profiles that follow are factual; in some instances I have provided historical ones, and in others I have shown you some African-Americans of today. The combination of historical and present-day examples will hopefully help you picture the application of the Nguzo Saba in a fuller chronology. Also, by using real people doing real things, I want to make it clear that the Seven Principles are practicable and within our reach. Whenever possible, my focus is on how Black women of varying ages and circumstances have exhibited the Nguzo Saba in some aspect of their lives. Please note this is not meant to exclude Black men. Rather, it is intended to give a glimpse of "herstory," and to inspire you to gather more examples of the wealth of role models for our young females. The Nguzo Saba are meant to guide us, enable us, and empower us to reclaim our role as contributors to world civilization. This is how some of us have put the Nguzo Saba into action:

UMOJA (Unity) — To strive for and maintain unity, with members of a family, community, nation, and race living together in peace and harmony.

Dalila Bentley is an adolescent sister who lives in Chicago, Illinois with her mother, father, and twin sister Jamila. Both of the Bentley children have written books to express their views on various topics that concern them, and they have emphasized the role of Christianity in their family life. Here is part of what Dalila wants you to know about the importance of understanding your family:

> One way to understand your family and your parents better is to have a family meeting. . . . What we do at our family meeting is we let out grudges and explain when we don't think something is fair. We don't spend the whole time arguing though. Family meetings are also discussion times. We tell our feelings.
> We try to let our parents know when they are doing a good job. We tell them we love them, because during the hardest times is when they need to hear it the most.[2]

Umoja is at work in the Bentleys' family life. By having family meetings, they give each other a chance to air problems and discuss them fully. It is also an avenue through which individual feelings are expressed within the collective arena of a family. Thus the oneness of a family is preserved alongside the development of each person. In addition, Dalila tells us how necessary it is to remember that love—especially during the hard times—should always be the perspective of a family life.

What can you do to promote umoja in the life of a Black female adolescent? Some possibilities include:

• Have a regular or spontaneous "hugging time" in which family members let go of whatever is troubling them in an atmosphere of love (this might also be a good way to end a family meeting).

• Suggest that family members or a tenants' group include a brief time period to "write it down and get it off your chest." During this period, participants might use writing as a tool to communicate their personal viewpoints, anonymously if necessary. Writing your grievances can give you a vehicle of expression and in the process of writing, you might verbalize your viewpoint more fully. The writings can then be shared within the group to stimulate further discussion as to similarities among views, how each viewpoint might promote a change in behavior, etc.

KUJICHAGULIA (Self-determination) — To make opportunities to name ourselves, define ourselves, create for ourselves, speak for ourselves, and make our own decisions instead of being named, defined, created, and spoken for by others who make decisions for us.

Ramona Hudson is another young Black female with whom I have been privileged to work. At the time of this profile, she was a student at the Alexandre Dumas School in Chicago, and she has been a regular participant in the writing workshops I conduct there. In 1987 she wrote this about herself:

"Me! I Get What I Want!"

I am a person. . . . I am Ramona Hudson and I get whatever I want. Nobody can stop me because when I want something I get it. For instance, I wanted to be an M & M [a hall guard]. I became one. I wanted to be on the second floor, I am. People don't know me very well, when I want something I get it. Like I wanted a pair of skates and I got them. When a person tells me, "You can't do that. You can't do this." I laugh and say, "Watch and see!"[3]

Ramona has been applying kujichagulia to her everyday world. She declares herself as someone for whom life presents a series of opportunities to be used, not shied from. She doesn't allow others to keep her from her goals and if she maintains this approach in the future, she will certainly succeed. This is the process of self-determination; it involves confidence, persistence, and self-love.

Kujichagulia can be activated in other ways. Some of those might be:

• Develop and promote methods for adolescent mothers to use in their contacts with the social service agencies with whom they often deal. Encourage young mothers to ask questions, take notes, and do follow-up phone calls if something isn't understood or if changes are desired or required. Then encourage them to discuss their dealings to focus on the process of choosing among alternatives when making decisions and to verbalize what those alternatives involve, the consequences of selecting one option versus another, etc.

• If a young Black female indicates an interest in writing, one way to apply kujichagulia to her writing is to suggest that she write a list of words or phrases that are positively "me" (her). If she only writes one or two at first, encourage her to add to the list on a regular basis. She might want to post the list on her bedroom wall, refrigerator door, or bathroom door so she can see it every day. Such a list reminds her that she can positively and specifically define herself.

One of the historical models of self-determination comes from the life of Sojourner Truth. She was born a slave in around 1797, and at first she was named Isabella Baumfree ("Bell"). However, she ran away, sued for the freedom of her child, won her case, worked as a domestic in New York City, and one day—inspired by a religious vision—walked away from her job, leaving all her possessions behind. She said she felt God had given her a mission to travel from place to place, declaring the truth wherever she went. She renamed herself Sojourner Truth. This Black heroine's life includes several examples of self-determination in action; one of the best known occurred at a women's rights meeting in 1851. Several men had attended the meeting with the sole purpose in mind of disrupting it. Also present was Sojourner Truth, whose support of equal rights for Blacks and women had already become well-known. During the meeting, Truth addressed the crowd:

> That man over there says that women need to be helped into carriages, and lifted over ditches, and to have the best place everywhere. Nobody ever helps me into carriages, or over mud-puddles, or gives me any best place! And ain't I a woman?...
> Then that little man over there, he says women can't have as much rights as men, 'cause Christ wasn't a woman! Where did your Christ come from? From God and a woman! Man had

nothing to do with Him.[4]

Sojourner Truth's bold words bring kujichagulia into forceful application. She makes it clear that the right to speak for oneself and participate in decision-making belongs to women as much as men. I often think of her when I hear about meetings in which critical policies are being shaped that will affect the lives of many Black females, and yet not one is there to speak for us. We all need to practice self-determination.

UJIMA (Collective Work and Responsibility) — To build and maintain our community, with everyone working together; to make our sisters' and brothers' problems our problems, and to solve them together so everyone survives.

One of the most effective examples of how ujima can work and young Black females can see it in action, is with mentorships. Mentorship programs vary a great deal in their focus and application, and they have been used with many different groups of mentors and mentees. However, the ultimate purpose of any mentorship is the bringing together of those with skills and resources that are needed by less experienced people who benefit from the sharing process.

I have been involved in such a program, which completed its pilot implementation in 1988. The program, called "Career Links," was initiated and sponsored by Women Employed, an organization designed to promote equal job opportunities and situations for women. Each of 28 Black women were given an equal number of Black female adolescents from various backgrounds and locations in Chicago. The program's main emphasis was to provide the adolescents an opportunity to see Black women at their various workplaces, and to gain further exposure to the working world through these visits as well as through group sessions that examined related issues, such as: tips on getting employment, and advice on the application process for college. Since the mentors' careers varied—for instance, some were in advertising, some in banking, and some were in public sector jobs—the mentees got a chance to meet Black women in diverse careers. In addition, I found that my relationship with my mentee brought me into closer contact with the world of adolescent Black females. As a result, I came to understand her and her peers much better. Thus for me the program caused a two-way growth to occur, and this is what I believe is essentially intended when ujima takes effect.

Another mentorship program, in Milwaukee, Wisconsin, approaches ujima in an interesting way. The "Each One/Reach One Program" began in 1981 and it is part of the New Concept Self Development Center.[5] Its director, June Martin Perry, uses the development of what she views as a primary tool —resourcefulness—as the vehicle for the mentorship. With resourcefulness as the goal, mentors are trained to identify and facilitate resources and access to them. Using the city, its services and community leaders as the "road map," mentors involve Black females ages seven to 17 in a series of methods designed to expose them to alternative lifestyles and help them make informed decisions. In addition, the mentors serve as positive role models by taking the young females to their job sites, to their homes, and to cultural events.

With resourcefulness as a tool to shape an alternative way of life, participation in "Each One/Reach One" brings ujima into effect. Being able to target and use resources in a community or city is essential to ujima because it automatically ties people and services to each other in a mutual way. When a Black adolescent female has a problem that needs solving or an interest she wants to develop, she will need resourcefulness to be effective. Thus ujima is difficult if impossible to achieve without resourcefulness.

Another approach to ujima can be found in peers themselves. This method is just getting underway on a more varied series of levels, and I think it will be successful in many instances. Peers have already been instituted in schools where they are used as tutors, and other situations include:

• Peers serve as counselors to Black adolescents, providing support and suggestions via telephone hotlines, in-school sessions, and after-school programs;

• A speakers bureau of trained youth who conduct discussion groups of teenagers on topics like pregnancy prevention, and coping with crises;

• Groups of young people who work within a school or neighborhood to serve as peer role models and who give programs designed to promote positive peer "pressure."

With approaches like these, Black female adolescents can gain a new perspective. Rather than seeing themselves as isolated individuals with no one to assist them, they can move toward a view that recognizes where and how connections can be made between themselves and the rest of their community.

UJAMAA (Cooperative Economics) — To build and maintain our own stores, shops, and other businesses, and to share the profits from them.

When it comes to economics, African-Americans have a tradition of sharing. We have long held food pantries, and we have often been cooperative about giving to the needy in our communities. On an informal or organizational level, ujamaa has been at work among us. There are some additional ways in which we can increase and enhance ujamaa in the lives of Black female adolescents.

One of them is a food co-op, in which a group of people organize and contribute their grocery budgets to buy food at a wholesale rate. Once purchased, the food items—as selected by each member—are distributed. With the lower wholesale rate used, the members save money. Such a co-op is in action at the Center for New Horizons in Chicago. Food co-ops are invaluable for additional reasons than saving money, though. Adolescent mothers or mothers-to-be must be especially conscious of the dietary needs of themselves and their children, and they often must do so on limited funds. Actually, all adolescent females need a healthy diet—this is a time in their lives when their physical development is greater than at any time since infancy. With participation in a food co-op, these segments of our population have the opportunity to maintain healthy diets while saving money.

Another reason for establishing a food co-op that focuses on adolescent needs is to promote an alternative dietary standard to the one so many of them use. Everyone knows about how popular fast and junk foods are to adolescents, so if a motivation is added to the food co-op—such as distributing the money saved among teens in exchange for their participation, or using the money saved to sponsor teens in the programs of their choice—it is possible that many of them will join. Their participation also could be very useful as workers in the co-op.

Churches have played roles that highlight ujamaa. One group of ministers in Chicago formed the Ministerial Advisory Council (MAC) in 1982 when a few ministers and the men's groups of their churches held a fund-raising breakfast. Since then, the council members have travelled to different high schools to conduct seminars on positive role identification and adolescent problem-solving methods. In terms of ujamaa, the council members hold fund-raising activities for various needs, one of which is transporation. It was discovered that some high school students were having trouble getting to school on a regular basis because they did not have the funds to use public transportation. Black adolescent mothers, it should be remembered, often have severely limited incomes; yet the federal government does not provide transportation allowances for impoverished teens. Thus it is ujamaa at work when a group like MAC steps in to seek a cooperative solution. In 1987, the Ministerial Advisory Council raised $2000 to be placed in an emergency transportation fund for students' use. With efforts like these, cooperative economics joins with academic opportunity to make a measurable difference in the lives of our Black youth.

Historically, our young Black females have some impressive role models of ujamaa in action. Black women formed a national movement of women's groups in the late 1800s and early 1900s. In every geographic location where we lived at that time, Black women formed clubs whose individual memberships varied in size, but whose devotion to community service made them larger than life. In 1895, Josephine St. Pierre Ruffin led the First National Conference of Colored Women; the same year, the National Federation of Afro-American Women formed, with Margaret Murray Washington as its president. Another organizing movement, the National League of Colored Women formed with Mary Church Terrell at the helm. In 1896, all these groups united to form the National Association of Colored Women.

The NACW used several methods to maintain cohesiveness and unity of purpose among the hundreds of clubs under its leadership. However, what is important in terms of ujamaa is the work of clubs at the local level. These were not primarily social groups; their major focus was on serving the communities in which they lived, and they often used cooperative economics to achieve their local goals. In 1896, the Washington, D.C. Colored Woman's League raised its own funds to establish and operate a training school for kindergarten teachers. For two years thereafter, the League operated seven free kindergartens. Their efforts were directed in this service because increasing numbers of Black women were working and the League realized the need to provide quality child care that had an educational orientation. It probably would have continued its efforts in this area had it not been for the fact that the city of Washington introduced kindergarten classes into the public school system. Clearly, ujamaa operated at the core of these sisters' focus and they used the money gained in the best interests of their peers and their families.

As part of its report to the 1906 national convention of Black women's clubs, the Sojourner Truth Club in Montgomery, Alabama outlined its activities. Among them was the establishment of a library, the first one that Blacks in that area ever had available to them. With a membership of 29 Black women, the club raised the funds to provide more than 300 books, magazines, tables, chairs, and every other item needed to furnish the library. As was stated in their report, "All this is paid for by 25 cents-per-month membership dues and fund-raising affairs held by the club."[6] In addition, guest speakers visited the reading room, including W.E.B. Dubois and Booker T. Washington. With just a few women and their determined fund raising, the gift of knowledge was provided to a community.

We have a history of cooperative economics and when it has been employed, the entire community has benefitted. In hundreds of ways—kindergartens, libraries, day nurseries, homes for the invalid, shelters for homeless girls—Black women have demonstrated their resourceful ability to find the money to serve their communities. Thus I find no reason to feel pessimistic about our present-day ability to use ujamaa, despite the reality of sometimes severe economic conditions. Regardless of the financial situation we find ourselves in, ujamaa will help us find our way to better times for our youth.

NIA (Purpose) — To make our collective vocation the building and developing of our community, and to do so in order to restore our people to their traditional greatness.

One of the reasons for the multitude of problems existing in our communities today is that we lack common goals and purposes. We live in a diversified society in which "freedom" has led many of us to overlook what we have in common. In many of the discussions that have occurred where Black female adolescents have been the topic, Blacks have sometimes concentrated so much on where we differ, the common elements have strayed from our attention. So nia is of great use to us, even as we realize it is also a challenge to apply.

In the area of education, our history provides significant models of nia at work. Mary McLeod Bethune, Lucy Laney, and Nannie Helen Burroughs are examples of such models. Each of them founded schools during the late 1800s to early 1900s, a period in which education was seen as a major goal for recently emancipated Blacks to achieve. Bethune founded the school named after her in 1906 in Daytona Beach, Florida; five Black girls, ages eight to 12, were her first pupils. At first there were so few funds, the students used burnt splinters as pencils and elderberry juice for ink. But Bethune had an abiding purpose which enabled her to continue her efforts. The school grew until a college for women was built, and in 1922 the Cookman College for Men united with her school to form Bethune-Cookman College.

Nannie Helen Burroughs, who was also an activist in the National Association of Colored Women's Clubs, believed in vocational training for women. She put her belief into action when she founded the National Training School in 1909. Twenty years later, Burroughs' school had eight buildings and 102 women and girls who were students. Her experience in raising the funds for the school was partly what prompted Burroughs to use the motto, "We specialize in the wholly impossible," to guide her in accomplishing what she saw as a necessary purpose: the "training of [Black women's] head, hand and heart and develop a definite and active social interest in the spiritual and moral forces that make for human welfare."[7]

The third educator I mentioned, Lucy Laney, founded Haines Normal School in Atlanta, Georgia in 1886. The school began with 75 students and by 1893, she pointed out:

> Through our forty student teachers, with schools now under their care that average 35 scholars each, we are reaching indirectly 1400 children. The three or four hundred added to this that come directly under our care causes us to reach about 1800 young people; but, oh, large as this number seems, it is small when we think of the many hundreds to whom scarcely a ray of light has yet come![8]

To Laney, her purpose in life was still to be accomplished. By 1940 because she kept to her goal of educating as many Blacks as she could, Laney's school had more than 1000 students. Like Bethune and Burroughs, she worked past many obstacles and continued her efforts. All three Black women kept their eyes on their goal; nothing distracted them and no one stopped them.

A variation of their motivation is seen today in a growing trend among Black women to form sisterhoods. These groups vary in size and specific function, according to their needs, location, and the availability of the members. Some are more oriented toward spiritual and emotional development, as is the case for the sisterhood that formed in 1988 at Trinity United Church of Christ in Chicago. Others, such as one that meets at Northeastern University in Chicago, are concerned with emotional development and also address social issues. The thread woven between these and other sisterhoods in New York City, Washington, D.C., and other areas, is the notion of commonly shared experiences. By promoting the linkages between Black females, a sisterhood helps to empower us on behalf of what is greater than us as individuals. In a sisterhood, a Black female develops a point of view that is collective in approach and oriented toward a community-based purpose.

KUUMBA (Creativity) — To do always as much as we can, in the way we can, to leave our community more beautiful and beneficial than we inherited.

The role of kuumba is essential to our cultural progress. With creativity that is focused on the beautification and benefit of the community as a whole, alternative messages can be expressed that combat the destructive images often presented by the dominant culture; Blacks with artistic talents have meaningful outlets that provide employment for them; and we are held accountable to future generations by the artistic forms we produce today. As such, kuumba is a political, social, emotional, and psychological tool, and its application has a tremendous effect on Black female youth.

One such group that has been putting kuumba to use is Sweet Honey in the Rock, six women who sing a cappella. The group was founded in 1973 through its members' participation in the Washington, D.C. Repertory Theatre; however, many of them, including the spokeswoman, Berniece Johnson Reagon, had been activists when they were Freedom Riders in the South. Since its formation, Sweet Honey in the Rock has performed its repertoire of work songs, folk songs, and songs about the struggle of Black people in the United States and Africa. As Reagon says, "When you're singing a song you're taking a political stance and you need to be called into account for that position."[9] Thus Sweet Honey in the Rock is a group of Black women who lend their voices to a greater understanding of important issues.

To hear this group of sisters perform is truly a lesson in kuumba. Their rich mixture of voices—across all the vocal ranges from soprano to bass—as well as the content of their songs, allows an audience to be entertained while learning some valuable messages. When Blacks like Sweet Honey in the Rock pursue kuumba, the community benefits from their messages and we need more groups like them.

There are many ways in which you can apply kuumba in your everyday life. A few suggestions are:

• Survey the classes offered at locations such as park fieldhouses, community centers, and community colleges, where the cost is low but you can get an introduction to the theory and practice of arts like pottery, photography, painting, or drawing. Make an effort to attend such classes and inform others about their existence—perhaps a small group can pool its funds to purchase supplies that can be shared so all may benefit.

• Encourage your neighbors or church members to pay for the services of an instructor in the arts. This is being done at some churches and senior citizen apartment buildings, and it allows greater access by bringing the instructor to her students. A situation of limited funds might be resolved by conducting a fund-raiser before and after the class sessions (in addition, the fund-raiser that follows the classes can feature the artistic creations as the items for sale). If more than one art form has been suggested, perhaps the classes can be alternated.

• Art forms are meant to be appreciated, so use every available environment to "show off" the latest creations of your daughter, your relatives, your neighbors, and yourself. Some ideas for environments that might become "galleries" are: the lobby of an apartment building, a meeting room at a church, the hallway of a school, etc.

IMANI (Faith) — To believe with all our heart in our people, our parents, our children, our teachers, our leaders, and in the righteousness and victory of our struggle.

The story of LyVonna Brown[10] reminds me of imani. She is a

17-year-old Chicagoan who has become an inventor. For five years, LyVonna has worked on her own laundry detergent, which she calls "LyVonna." When she began, she was conducting experiments for a science fair project; however, she has continued to test her product against other brand-name detergents. As a result of her efforts, LyVonna has won school and regional competitions, and the attention of Willie Morrissett, who "adopted" her as part of the "Adopt a High School Student" program at the University of Illinois-Chicago. Through this program, LyVonna pursues advanced studies in chemistry at the University of Illinois which will allow her to gain additional mastery of a subject in which she has already demonstrated great interest.

Imani is part of LyVonna's success story, because it took faith in herself and her idea to realize that she could invent a product. Working on an idea for five years requires persistence and persistence is built on faith. LyVonna must have known she needed persistence; she entered her laundry detergent experiments in each science fair from the seventh to the tenth grade. Each year, she increased the number of tests she conducted so she could establish more detailed information about her product. This is the kind of pursuit of a scientific goal which George Washington Carver maintained during his many years of experiments. If she maintains her faith in herself, LyVonna has what it takes to become an effective scientist.

As it so happens, LyVonna attends a church that undoubtedly enhances her ability to practice imani. The church is Trinity United Church of Christ in Chicago, and it offers a wealth of services and programs for all segments of its congregation. Among the opportunities that might interest a Black female youth are: an employment ministry, a young adult ministry, the "Adopt a Student" ministry which is targeted at students attending college away from home, a food sharing program, choir, Bible study, and "Sojourner Truth," an afternoon series of seminars and workshops specifically for young Black females.

In addition to these programs, there are numerous others for other age groups. In fact, there are so many services offered at Trinity that it represents a church with truly an "open door" policy in action. In Chapter Two, I pointed out the need for Black churches to re-orient their approach toward Black adolescents. Imani makes a new outreach possible. Imani is what Nannie Burroughs had when she said, "We specialize in the wholly impossible." Without imani, the situation facing Black adolescent females seems "wholly impossible." Imani makes all things possible so the needs of our young females can be met.

A RITES OF PASSAGE PROGRAM FOR YOU

In this chapter, a rites of passage program is provided for you to use with a selected group of Black female adolescents. Many variations of rites of passage exist in traditional African societies.[1] Generally, a rite of passage is an initiation of a young person into adulthood. Sometimes there is one main ceremony marking the official acceptance of the youth into her or his society. In other groups, there are several progressively more difficult activities that a youth must accomplish to reach a final initiation.

Preparation is the key to being initiated into Black female adulthood; it is one of the major elements of African beliefs which succeeded in making its way through the generations of African-American females. Therefore, the program outlined in this chapter takes that into account. In addition, since so many needs exist among modern Black female youth, an attempt has been made here to use the "serial" approach to rites of Black female passage. That being the case, there is no single rite of passage promoted in this program, but a series of inter-related rites of passage. With this program as a model, I hope to stimulate approaches that are tailored to a specific community of Black female adolescents.

This chapter is divided into four sections so you will obtain a holistic view of the program. What follows are:

• the overall objectives of the Black female rites of passage

program outlined in this chapter;
* five administrative phases and questions to consider during each phase;
* the components of the "curriculum," in which six areas are explored;
* supplementary areas that provide ideas to help you adapt the program's components to the needs of your participants, and to give you ways to expand the program over time or among additional groups.

Overall Objectives

The overall objectives of this rites of passage program are:
1. To foster knowledge among young Black females of the specific nature of their sexuality;
2. To encourage appreciation of African-American familyhood and the manner in which process-oriented, survival-based family roles are shaped by cultural traditions and individual circumstances;
3. To enhance participants' awareness of their role in the development of their community and their friendships;
4. To increase the appropriate and practical use of time, work habits, and money;
5. To direct participants' interests and attitudes toward creative self-expression as a meaningful vehicle;
6. To use nurturing, self-loving approaches to a variety of everyday as well as "benchmark" situations.
OVERALL GOAL: To provide opportunities for Black female adolescents to prepare themselves—physically, socially, emotionally, intellectually, and culturally—for passage to womanhood.

Administering the Program

Listed here are five phases related to administering a rites of passage program. These phases are:
1) Assess and Adapt—Plan how the program will proceed by taking stock of the overall situation (that is, where it will be held, who will help you in terms of "teachers" and other staff, how often will it be held, etc.) as well as the specific ways you will adapt the program (which segments will remain as is, which parts need changing according to your specific situation, etc.);
2) Recruit—Prepare the steps necessary to inform potential participants of the upcoming program;

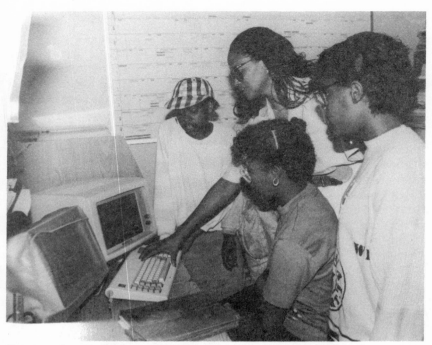

Preparation is the key to initiating them into womanhood.

3) Introduce—Make the necessary provisions to enable you to introduce the program in an informative and meaningful way;

4) Implement—Carry out the program according to the manner in which you adapted it;

5) Evaluate—Check on the progress of the program in terms of its operation versus the overall objectives.

Generally, these phases pertain to administering any program. However, it is possible that this program will be used by people with less administrative experience than others. The following questions are meant as ones to ask yourself, regardless of your administrative expertise. In addition, the questions are guidelines to which you should add whatever other concerns you need to address in terms of your specific situation. You might want to keep these questions in mind as you proceed.

1) Assess and Adapt
—What are the available facilities that might serve as the site of the program? Which ones seem most preferable and why?

117

—What flexibility do you have in the host facility? Is the place so crowded with use by your and other groups that, should a scheduling change become necessary, you might risk losing the use of the facility?

—Where is the host facility located in reference to the youth you want to serve? Is there a possibility they might have to cross dangerous areas to reach the host facility? If so, how might this affect your scheduling?

—Have the appropriate adults been contacted and have they signed on their support of the program's concept if not its implementation?

—Do you know who the host facility's chain of command are, and the facility's specific safety procedures to follow in event of an emergency? Is insurance a necessity?

—Do you have parental consent forms drawn up for any participants who are minors?

—Have you put together a budget for any supplies or materials that will be used in the program? Do you need to raise funds to make the budget a reality, or will you seek other monetary resources (such as charging a small fee from participants)?

—What general information do you have about the Black female youth in your area? How many can you reasonably involve?

—Given your resources of time, facility, and money, what elements of the rites of passage program will you be able to implement? How will this affect your expectations and the overall objectives?

2) Recruit

—What avenues will you pursue to recruit participants—block clubs, neighborhood churches and schools, social service agencies in the neighborhood, neighborhood newspapers?

—How will you limit your recruiting if the community's population of Black female youth is too large to accommodate?

—How do you plan to involve parents in the recruitment process—by introducing the program first to them, or by bringing parents into the process after participants are chosen?

—Over what period of time will you conduct your recruitment—two weeks, three weeks, a month?

—What kind of follow-up will you do to ensure awareness of the program—phone, mail, personal visits?

3) Introduce
—What provisions have been made to introduce the program in a flexible manner (such as more than one session, more than one place, more than one time period) to accomodate different scheduling needs?

—Who will introduce the program and what aspects of it will be presented?

—Will parents be invited to the introductory session(s), and if so, has their attendance been taken into account in terms of the time and day of the session?

4) Implement
—Who will implement the program's components, and how have they been involved in assessment, adaptation, recruitment, and introduction?

—Is the number of implementors versus the number of participants appropriate to this program? Is the ratio reasonable for appropriate attention and adequate supervision of activities?

—Is there consensus among the implementors regarding the program's components and objectives?

—Is there any mechanism in place for implementors to give ongoing feedback (such as questionnaires, meetings, a "complaint box," or a "suggestion box")?

—Is there any mechanism in place for participants to give ongoing feedback?

5) Evaluate
—At what point will you evaluate the program? Every three months? Every six months? On a yearly basis?

—What methods will you use for evaluation—anonymous questionnaires, meetings, a combination of methods?

—What elements (components, schedule, staff) will you evaluate and why?

—Who will be held accountable for what emerges from the evaluation?

—What provisions will be made for revising the program if evaluation indicates this is preferable or necessary?

Program Components

The six components of the Black female rites of passage

program are:
1) Sexuality
2) Familyhood
3) Our Community/Our Friends
4) Our Time/Our Work/Our Money
5) The Well of Creativity
6) Being and Becoming Whole and Proud

It is suggested that these components be implemented on a consecutive basis. As a whole, the program is estimated to require a year to complete if sessions are held on a twice weekly basis.

SEXUALITY

Overall Objective: To foster knowledge among participants of the specific nature of Black female sexuality.

Goals:

1. To increase knowledge of the stages of adolescent growth.
2. To increase knowledge of the areas of development within each stage.
3. To specify participant's concrete reasons for delaying the onset of sexual intercourse.
4. To specify participant's concrete reasons for delaying pregnancy.
5. To increase awareness of myths about Black females and the role of myth-making today.
6. To facilitate formation of personal definitions of Black female sexuality.

Methods:

1. Present and discuss relevant details regarding preadolescence, mid-adolescence, and late adolescence.
2. Present and discuss information related to areas of development: physical, intellectual, social, and emotional.
3A. Review major points learned about four areas of development.
3B. Brainstorm various developmental consequences of sexual intercourse during each stage of adolescence.
4A. Summarize health-related problems and risks for adolescent pregnancy.
4B. Discuss other developmental consequences of adolescent pregnancy.

5A. Analyze examples of Black female myths from popular media.
5B. Summarize history of myths about Black females.
6A. Review myth-making about Black females.
6B. Brainstorm list of elements of identity.
6C. Personalize a definition of Black female sexuality.

Resources:

1) Film detailing adolescent growth stages
2) Health Care Professionals
3) Booklets from Children's Defense Fund or local health clinic specifying health-related risks of early sexual intercourse
4) Film examining consequences of adolescent pregnancy
5A) Photographs and advertisements from fashion and current events magazines; record album jackets featuring popular Black female entertainers
5B) Articles[2] examining historical myth-making about Black females
6) Program implementor

Outcomes:

1. & 2.—Written summaries and notes
3.—Individual lists of short-term and long-term goals
4.—Role-playing about decision-making process regarding pregnancy
5.—Group discussion identifying elements of myth-making
6A.—Brainstormed list of elements identifying a Black female (small groups)
6B.—Individual lists defining Black female sexuality

FAMILYHOOD

Overall Objective: To encourage appreciation of African-American familyhood and the manner in which process-oriented, survival-based roles are shaped by cultural traditions and individual circumstances.

Goals:

1. To increase knowledge of African traditions regarding family roles.
2. To develop awareness of participant's responsibility and

importance to her family's effectiveness.

3. To demonstrate at least one way participant can apply an African tradition to the life of her family.

Methods:

1. Present and discuss information about family roles in African societies.

2A. Analyze various family activities.

2B. Compare and contrast structure versus process in family roles.

3. Identify African traditions related to young Black females.

Resources:

1) Films or slides about societies such as Ashanti and Yoruba

2A) Participants and implementor

2B) Chapter Two of this book; article "Africanity" by Wade Nobles[3]

3) Same resources listed in #1 above

Outcomes:

1.—Group chart outlining family roles in African societies

2.—Diary of family roles and personal responsibilities

3A.—Invitations to family event

3B.—Family event, e.g., African meal

OUR COMMUNITY/OUR FRIENDS

Overall Objective: To enhance participants' awareness of their role in the development of their community and their friendships.

Goals:

1. To develop specific definitions of participant's expectations regarding her community and her friend's roles in her life.

2. To increase awareness of participant's responsibility, role, and importance to her community and friends.

3. To increase skills in implementing participant's community role.

4. To increase knowledge of role a community has played in African-American history.
5. To facilitate development of communication skills.

Methods:

1A. Discuss ways in which participant indicates what she wants from her community.
1B. Identify situations which indicate participant's expectations of her friendship role.
2. Summarize specific responsibilities toward community and friends.
3. Summarize areas in which participant can be an educated consumer.
4. Present and discuss community-based events in African-American history (e.g., school desegregation, community business boycotts, etc.).
5. Identify process of communication among peers.

Resources:

1) Directories of community organizations
2) Community leaders; participants
3A) Film on consumerism
3B) Consumer guides (magazines and books)
4) Books, e.g., *The Black Woman,*[4] *Black Women in White America,*[5] *The Long Shadow of Little Rock*[6]
5) Program implementor

Outcomes:

1.—Group list of services provided by community; individual summaries of situations regarding participants' friendship role
2A.—Individual lists of questions to ask community leaders
2B.—Written summaries of interviews conducted
2C.—Individual lists of responsibilities toward friends
3.—Role plays involving consumer situations
4.—Group debate about historical role of African-American communities versus today
5.—Small group discussions regarding issues of communication between friends

OUR TIME/OUR WORK/OUR MONEY

Overall Objective: To increase the appropriate and practical use of time, work habits, and money.

Goals:

1. To increase awareness of role of time in adult life.
2. To increase knowledge of work habits participant can presently implement.
3. To foster awareness of ways to implement cooperative economics.

Methods:

1. Present and discuss situations emphasizing time as adults use it.
2A. Identify participant's present work habits.
2B. Compare present work habits to adult concept of time.
2C. Identify goals of work habits to presently use versus those to develop into job skills for the short- or long-term future.
3A. Review consumer information gained in "OUR COMMUNITY" section.
3B. Discuss ideas for group project (e.g., bake sale, used book or toy sale, recycled newspapers or bottles to sell).
3C. Identify ways to implement cooperative economics (e.g., use profit from project for supplies for next component, use profit to join or begin food co-op, put profit back into repeat of project).

Resources:

1A) Examples of job application or questionnaire asking about participant's present job skills
1B) Stopwatch or timer
2A) Diary of family roles/personal responsibilities from "FAMILYHOOD" section
2B) Implementor
2C) Book in which job skills are classified by career
3A) Directory of community services and businesses
3B) Small business owner from community
3C) Program implementor

Outcomes:

1.—Group game in which participants complete written exercise (questionnaire asking for list of skills each participant believes would gain her a job at present; or a sample job application); participants are timed as to how long it takes to complete exercise
2A.—Individual brainstormed lists of work habits
2B.—Small group discussion of comparing individual work habits to time concept discovered from group game
2C.—Written goals of new work habits to pursue and "old" work habits to reinforce
3A. Small group lists of community needs
3B. Group interview of small business owner
3C. Outline of group project to pursue

THE WELL OF CREATIVITY

Overall Objective: To direct participants' interests and attitudes toward creative self-expression as a meaningful vehicle.

Goals:

1. To increase participant's awareness of African traditions in music, crafts, and dance.
2. To foster participant's interest in gaining additional skills in African-oriented music, crafts, or dance.
3. To increase knowledge of ways in which African arts traditions are applied to popular arts
4. To facilitate production of alternative "media messages" involving music, crafts, or dance.

Methods:

1. Present and identify styles and characteristics of African music, crafts, and dance forms.
2A. Identify individual interests in the arts.
2B. Participate in instructional session in either of three areas (music, dance, or crafts).
2C. Identify ideas for presentation of skills learned.
3. Present and discuss characteristics of popular music and dance.
4A. Identify ways in which popular media characterize music, dance, and crafts.

4B. Discuss alternative possibilities for promoting arts through various media.

Resources:

1A) Records of traditional African songs
1B) Photographs of African pottery and jewelry
1C) African dance instructor
2) Museum staff person specializing in African arts, or dance instructor, craftsmakers, and musicians
3A) Books about African arts, or resources from #1 and #2
3B) Photographs of advertisements from general and arts magazines
3C) Examples from popular arts, e.g., rap records, jewelry, dance steps, etc.
4A) Photographs from #3B)
4B) Program implementor

Outcomes:

1.—Group chart of styles and characteristics of African art forms
2.—Attendance at instructional session or museum visit featuring at least one art form
3.—Written summaries of attributes from African arts being applied in popular arts today
4.—"Alternative media exhibit" featuring promotional products (e.g., newsletter, bulletin board, taped jingle, rap)

BEING AND BECOMING WHOLE AND PROUD

Overall Objective: To use nurturing, self-loving approaches to a variety of everyday as well as "benchmark" situations.

Goals:
1. To increase awareness of nurturing techniques to use in everyday situations.
2. To increase knowledge of "benchmark" events in a Black female's life.
3. To demonstrate skills gained throughout the rites of passage program.

Methods:
1A. Present and discuss characteristics of nurturing behavior.

126

1B. Identify and discuss attributes of African values.
2. Identify and discuss examples of "benchmark" situations in participant's present and future life.
3A. Review outcomes from previous five components.
3B. Identify specific outcomes for final, initiation ceremony.
3C. Plan initiation ceremony.

Resources:

1) Program implementor; books about African values and philosophies[7]
2) Goals listed in outcomes of "SEXUALITY," "FAMILYHOOD," "OUR TIME," "COMMUNITY/FRIENDS," and "CREATIVITY" sections
3) Books about initiation ceremonies[8]; program implementor

Outcomes:

1.—Individual journals describing approaches to everyday situations, and ways to apply new expectations of self-love
2.—Small group lists of "benchmark" events (e.g., graduation from school, first job, marriage, first home of one's own, first date, etc.)
3A.—Invitations to initiation ceremony
3B.—Participation in ceremony of each participant's outcomes in at least one component area (e.g., group booklet of selected summaries, lists and diary/journal entries; alternative media messages; dance routine; crafts exhibit)

Supplements to the Program

Supplementary ideas are presented here which you might want to implement to increase involvement by participants in the rites of passage program. The ideas are meant to enhance the foundation of objectives provided in the program, in order to give participants additional opportunities to engage in meaningful activities together, use their free time in beneficial ways, and increase the likelihood of absorbing what they have learned.

Another possible application of the supplementary segment is to operate two programs simultaneously: in this kind of situation, one segment—the rites of passage program—would involve one set of participants, while the other segment—the supplementary program—would have another set of participants. In that way, two populations are benefitting from the

Sports activity should always be paired with education.

overall objectives, and each group can exchange program involvements after a given period.

Finally, the supplementary suggestions might be used by themselves. In situations in which a limitation of funds does not allow implementing the rites of passage program, or if you simply prefer to just implement the supplements, be assured that each idea is based on actual programs already in existence elsewhere. At any rate, it might be helpful for you to refer to the "Administering the Program" section of this chapter if you use these program ideas. Please feel free to make your own adaptations.

Her Sports, Her Life

This supplementary program is based partly on those developed by Dr. Larry Hawkins of the Office of Special Programs, University of Chicago; and on a program sponsored by the Men of Shiloh Baptist Church, Washington, D.C. It has two components:

1. *Sports Activity.* Participants will be allowed to engage regularly in a group sport, such as volleyball, basketball, track, or a sport you select. At the beginning of implementation, it is advisable to find out the level of proficiency of the sport. (Among younger adolescents especially, basic information may need to be provided about the sport.)

In addition, participants will be given opportunities at regular intervals to engage in either intramural or inter-team competition. An awards ceremony should include recognition of outstanding effort and/or proficiency gained in the sports activity component.

2. *Sports Education.* This component would focus on the academic aspects of sports in America. Small groups (or "teams") might be formed to gather information about Black female athletes—past and present, well-known and community-based —as well as the role and effects of Blacks' participation in American sports, for the purpose of presenting the information to the whole group. Ideas for presentation might include: 1) inviting athletes to speak and be interviewed; 2) creating a board or question/answer game using the information found; 3) conducting a sports education conference in which each group participates in roundtable discussions about: characteristics of a successful Black female athlete, the effect of Black female athletes as role models, the effect of racism and sexism on the development of Black female athletes, etc.

NOTE: It is strongly advisable that participation in the education component be made mandatory to participation in the activity component. Involvement in one should not exclude involvement in the other, and the education component would greatly reinforce the attributes (discipline, preparation, persistence, etc.) needed for the activity component.

Creatively Resourceful

This program is designed to engage Black female adolescents in a series of activities that will broaden their perspective toward the arts. It is also meant to bring them closer to the African-based view of the arts as an everyday necessity.

1. *Creative Activity.* This component involves various avenues for activating informal levels of curiosity about arts-related situations. Participants are encouraged to use the materials around them (such as scrap metal; secondhand toys; dried flowers or leaves; dried, hollowed-out shells of squash; fabric remnants; dime store notions; inexpensive kitchen utensils, etc.) to "create" or "invent" useful items for cooking, cleaning, personal apparel, and recreation. Some examples of ways to create such items are: toys for pets or relatives,

jewelry, pot holders, musical instruments, book marks, etc. (other examples might be found in a book about recyclable materials, or a children's craft book).

2. *Resource Education.* This component fosters greater understanding of participants' role in their communities as resource seekers and resource enhancers. A variety of approaches might be considered useful: as resource seekers, small teams of two or three participants could gather various items—such as directories of community services and businesses (including those related to the arts), brochures about organizations and events in the community (including those with an arts focus), maps of the area—or the teams could gather the information about services, businesses, organizations and events, and the location of these community resources, and use the information for the next task: being resource enhancers. In this role, participants are encouraged to implement what they have learned about community resources. Possibilities include: making a community directory and selling it to raise funds for future program activities; making a brochure about themselves as community resource persons who can help peers gain better access to community resources and how to use them; or having a special program about community resources, to which peers are invited to learn more about community resources.

AFTERWORD

"Be not discouraged black women of the world, but push forward, regardless of the lack of appreciation shown you."

—Amy-Jacques Garvey
October 24, 1925

This is a time when Amy-Jacques Garvey's words ring true for all Black females, including adolescents. Young Black females face a multitude of obstacles in their path. Poverty, racism, sexism, violence, and other difficulties present seemingly insurmountable barriers to the future they deserve to anticipate eagerly. At this time in their lives, when they are by nature susceptible to environmental influences, they need strong approaches to cope with the present and shape the future.

The measures that many of them are presently using appear to be largely inadequate or worse, distinctly wrong. The aggressiveness that is becoming a pattern of behavior among some, and the continuance of taking on lifestyles like adolescent motherhood among others, are indications of ways in which young Black females attempt to deal with their environment. Those who adopt such behaviors and lifestyles are not "deviant"; on one level they are using the worldliness and resourcefulness noted by Joyce Ladner in her book *Tomorrow's Tomorrow*. In other words, it is their way of telling the world, "You handed me this confusing, contradictory mess and gave me little if any means of handling it. I'm trying to deal with it the best way I know how."

Yet those of us who look ahead realize how much they endanger their futures and the continuance of our culture. The increasingly younger ages of engaging in sexual intercourse and the large number of adolescent mothers—some of whom have more than one child while still in their teens—and the widening gap between those at the poverty level and those who are making middle-class incomes, demonstrate that we have a great deal of work to do with them and for them. For

131

without strong intervention taking place now, the cycle is likely to repeat itself among greater numbers of Black female adolescents.

The work that must be done begins within Black adults. We must confront our failure to model healed, varied relationships with our peers—male and female. We also have not reached a consensus about our self-images and the importance of African-American culture in our lives and those of our young people. These gaps have been critical to the ways in which we might have handled difficulties like inadequate incomes, housing shortages, child care, and the myriad other troubles compounding the struggle to become an adult.

So we all have quite a bit of work to do. There is no better time than the present to establish complete selves and to encourage situations which make it possible for our youth to do so as well. While the "work" is complex, it is also an exciting, dynamic challenge, full of possibilities as to what can be accomplished if self-actualization is viewed as an achievable goal. The process of grappling with this goal is manageable, and I hope I have stimulated some ideas to emerge within you. We have an opportunity to engage in a righteous journey that will result in no less than the restoration of our leading role in the world. As you know, when we as a people and as individuals decide to accomplish something meaningful, we have succeeded before. If we can recreate the level of the role we once held when we built outstanding civilizations in Africa, there is no limit to what can be built anew.

I bring up Africa because it serves as a foundation of ideals, values, and achievements for us to model and reshape in the situation we face now. Geraldine Wilson, an outstanding role model of a sister who was dedicated to renewed and creative methods of child development, reminded me of the need to reclaim our ties to our homeland:

> Our relationship to African women is not as far away and as much a part of our "memories" as white historians (and some of ours) have tried to make it. It's been close enough to reach out and touch. It's had impact on our upbringing as children. Let's catch it before it's too late and let's have one of our own take us back in time.[1]

I invite you to lead our Black women-to-be along their most important journey—to the role of womanhood that will recreate us as a people.

FOOTNOTES

Foreword

1. Mary McLeod Bethune, "A Century of Progress of Negro Women," *Black Women in White America, A Documentary History*, Gerda Lerner (ed.), New York: Vintage Books, 1972, p. 583.

Chapter One

1. Many of the comments and vignettes in this chapter are from the "1988 Black Youth Survey," which the author wrote and administered. A total of 118 respondents participated and several different surveys were administered on subjects such as relationships with family members, love and sex, being Black, being female, the neighborhood and free time, etc. Confidentiality was ensured, so none of the respondents' names are identified here. For further details regarding this survey, please contact the publisher.
2. Descriptions of the three adolescent stages and the areas of growth are based on: Children's Defense Fund, *Opportunities for Prevention: Building After-School and Summer Programs for Young Adolescents* (Washington, D.C.: Children's Defense Fund, July 1987), p. 14; and Louise J. Kaplan, *Adolescence: The Farewell to Childhood* (New York: Simon and Schuster, 1984), pp. 130-133.
3. *Webster's New Collegiate Dictionary* (Springfield: G. & C. Merriam Company, 1973), pp. 1054-1055.
4. Joyce Ladner, *Tomorrow's Tomorrow, The Black Woman* (Garden City: Doubleday, 1971), p. 109.
5. Ladner, *Tomorrow's Tomorrow*, p. 175.
6. Francis Cress Welsing, "The Cress Theory of Color Confrontation," 1970; and speech given by Francis Cress Welsing, Center for Inner City Studies, April 30, 1988.
7. Mary Burgher, "Images of Self and Race in the Autobiographies of Black Women," *Sturdy Black Bridges, Visions of Black Women in Literature*, Roseann P. Bell, Bettye J. Parker, and Beverly Guy-Sheftall (eds.), Garden City: Anchor Books, 1979, p. 111.

Chapter Two

1. Mary C. Lewis, 1972, unpublished.
2. "Mrs. James" was encountered by the author during a visit to an elementary school in Chicago; "Mrs. Washington" and some of the situation on which her story is based resulted from an interview the author conducted at a health clinic in Chicago.
3. Wade Nobles, "Africanity: Its Role in Black Families," *The Black Family: Essays and Studies*, Robert Staples (ed.), Belmont: Wadsworth, 1978, p. 22.
4. Nobles, p. 22.
5. Nobles, p. 24.
6. Ernestine Mason, "Still Tomboys or Credible Athletes?" *School Sports & Education*, 2:1, Spring 1986, p. 21.
7. Interview with Dr. Larry Hawkins, June 1, 1988.
8. By the phrase "Moynihan reactions," the author is referring to the controversy caused by the perspective that dominated in the book by Daniel Moynihan, *The Negro Family: The Case for National Action* (Washington: Government Printing Office, 1965). One of the criticisms of this book involved the implication that Black families were mainly "deviant" because Moynihan noted the existence of many female-headed households among Black families.
9. Jo-Ellen Asbury, "African-American Women in Violent Relationships: An Exploration of Cultural Differences," *Violence in the Black Family: Correlates and Consequences*, Robert L. Hampton (ed.), Lexington: DC Heath, 1987, pp. 96-7.
10. Nobles, p. 22.
11. The Drug Abuse Warning Network, *Trends in Drug Abuse Related Hospital Emergency Room Episodes and Medical Examiner Cases for Selected Drugs* (Washington, D.C.: National Institute on Drug Abuse, U.S. Public Health Service, 1986), pp. 53 and 288.
12. Nannie H. Buurroughs, "Glorify Blackness," *Black Women in White America*, p. 552.

Chapter Three

1. Asbury, p. 97.
2. Address by Dr. Jerome L. Schulman, Chairman, Department of Psychiatry, Children's Memorial Hospital, at Conference on Pre-Adolescence, Chicago Department of Health, Chicago, Illinois, March 11, 1988.
3. Schulman, Conference on Pre-Adolescence.
4. Ralph Ellison, *Going to the Territory* (New York: Vantage, 1986), p. 52.

5. Christine Carrington, "Depression Among African-American Women," *The Black Woman*, La Frances Rodgers-Rose (ed.), Beverly Hills: Sage Publications, 1980, p. 267.
6. Janet Singleton, *Sisters* (Lakewood: RAJ Publications/Rocky Mountain Planned Parenthood, 1979), n.p.
7. Barbara J. Callaway, "Women in Ghana," *Women in the World*, Lynne B. Iglitzin and Ruth Ross (eds.), Santa Barbara: Clio Books, 1976, p. 192.
8. Marian Wright Edelman, *Families in Peril: An Agenda for Social Change* (Cambridge: Harvard University Press, 1987), pp. 2-3.
9. Mary C. Lewis, 1973, unpublished.

Chapter Four

1. Maulana Karenga, "Social Ethics and the Black Family, An Alternative Analysis," *The Black Scholar*, September/October 1986, p. 51.

Chapter Five

1. "The History of Kwanzaa," *Ebony Jr!*, December 1982, p. 10.
2. Dalila Bentley, "Family Meetings," *Adolescent Girls in Christ* (Chicago: The Bentleys, 1987), p. 8.
3. Ramona Hudson, "I'm Me! I Get What I Want!" *Young Authors of Dumas, A 1987 Anthology by Students at Alexandre Dumas Elementary School*, Mary C. Lewis (ed.), Chicago: Mary C. Lewis/Chicago Office of Fine Arts, 1987, p. 10; used by permission of the Chicago Office of Fine Arts.
4. *Narrative of Sojourner Truth: A Bondswoman of Olden Time*, Olive Gilbert, comp. (New York: Arno Press, 1968 [1878]), pp. 133-4.
5. For more details regarding "Each One/Reach One," see Children's Defense Fund, *Model Programs: Preventing Adolescent Pregnancy and Building Youth Self-Sufficiency*, Washington, D.C.: Children's Defense Fund, July 1986.
6. "Sojourner Truth Club of Montgomery, Alabama," *Black Women in White America, A Documentary History*, p. 453.
7. "The National Training School for Girls Appeals for Funds," *Black Women in White America*, p. 133.
8. "A Progress Report from the Founder of the Haines School," *Black Women in White America*, p. 123.

9. Televised interview of Berneice J. Reagon, *Ebony/Jet Showcase*, April 24, 1988.
10. Based on profile of LyVonna Brown, "Trailblazer," *Inteen*, Dr. Colleen Birchett, ed., Chicago: Urban Ministries, September/October/November 1988, inside back cover.

Chapter Six

1. For information regarding African rites of passage and their role in African societies, see: R. Radcliffe Brown and Daryl Forde, *African Systems of Kinship and Marriage* (New York: Oxford University Press, 1967); Arnold van Gennep, *The Rites of Passage* (Chicago: University of Chicago Press, 1960); and Monika Vizedom, *Rites and Relationships* (Beverly Hills: Sage Publications, 1976).
2. See: Mary Burgher, "Images of Self and Race in the Autobiographies of Black Women," *Sturdy Black Bridges, Visions of Black Women in Literature* (Bell, Parker, Guy-Sheftall, eds.), Garden City: Anchor Books, 1979, pp. 107-22; Mae C. King, "The Politics of Sexual Stereotypes," *Black Scholar*, March/April 1973, pp. 12-23.
3. See: Wade Nobles, "Africanity: Its Role in Black Families," *The Black Family: Essays and Studies*, Robert Staples (ed.), Belmont: Wadsworth, 1978, pp. 19-26.
4. La Frances Rodgers-Rose, ed., *The Black Woman* (Beverly Hills: Sage Publications, 1980).
5. Gerda Lerner, ed., *Black Women in White America* (New York: Vintage Books, 1972).
6. Daisy Lee Bates, *The Long Shadow of Little Rock* (New York: David McKay, 1962).
7. See: Cheikh Anta Diop, *The Cultural Unity of Negro Africa* (Paris: Presence Africaine, 1963); John S. Mbiti, *African Religions and Philosophies* (New York: Anchor, 1970); Wade Nobles, "African Philosophy: Foundations for Black Psychology," *Black Psychology*, Reginald Jones (ed.), New York: Harper & Row, 1972; and G. K. Osei, *The African Philosophy of Life* (London: The African Publican Society, 1970).
8. See: Radcliffe R. Brown and Daryl Forde, *African Systems of Kinship and Marriage*; Arnold van Gennep, *The Rites of Passage*; and Monika Vizedom, *Rites and Relationships*.

Afterword

1. Geraldine L. Wilson, "The Self/Group Actualization of Black Women," *The Black Woman*, p. 309.

SELECTED BIBLIOGRAPHY

Books

Angelou, Maya. *I Know Why the Caged Bird Sings.* New York: Random House, 1970.

Bambara, Toni Cade. *Gorilla My Love.* New York: Random House, 1972.

Bates, Daisy Lee. *The Long Shadow of Little Rock.* New York: David McKay, 1962.

Bell, Roseann P.; Parker, Bettye J.; and Guy-Sheftall, Beverly; ed. *Sturdy Black Bridges: Visions of Black Women in Literature.* Garden City: Anchor, 1979.

Children's Defense Fund. *Child Care: An Essential Service for Teen Parents.* Washington, D.C.: Children's Defense Fund, March 1987.

_____. *Model Programs: Preventing Adolescent Pregnancy and Building Youth Self-Sufficiency.* Washington, D.C.: Children's Defense Fund, July 1986.

_____. *Opportunities for Prevention: Building After-School and Summer Programs for Young Adolescents.* Washington, D.C.: Children's Defense Fund, July 1987.

_____. *Preventing Adolescent Pregnancy: What Schools Can Do.* Washington, D.C.: Children's Defense Fund, September 1986.

_____. *Welfare and Teen Pregnancy: What Do We Know? What Do We Do?* Washington, D.C.: Children's Defense Fund, November 1986.

Diop, Cheikh Anta. *African Origin of Civilization: Myth or Reality.* Westport: Lawrence Hill, 1974.

_____. *The Cultural Unity of Negro Africa.* Paris: Presence Africaine, 1963.

Giddings, Paula. *When and Where I Enter: The Impact of Black Women on Race and Sex in America.* New York: Morrow, 1984.

Hale-Benson, Janice. *Black Children: Their Roots, Culture and Learning Styles.* Baltimore: Johns Hopkins University Press, 1982.

Hull, Gloria T.; Scott, Patricia Bell; and Smith, Barbara; eds. *But Some of Us Are Brave.* New York: The Feminist Press, 1982.

Kunjufu, Jawanza. *Developing Positive Self-Images and Discipline in Black Children.* Chicago: African American Images, 1984.

Ladner, Joyce. *Tomorrow's Tomorrow: The Black Woman.* Garden City: Doubleday, 1971.

Lerner, Gerda, ed. *Black Women in White America: A Documentary History.* New York: Vintage, 1972.

McCray, Walter. *Reaching and Teaching Black Young Adults.* Chicago: Black Light Fellowship, 1986.

Rodgers-Rose, La Francis, ed. *The Black Woman.* Beverly Hills: Sage Publications, 1980.

Washington, Mary Helen, ed. *Black-Eyed Susans: Classic Stories by and about Black Women.* Garden City: Doubleday, 1975.

Articles

Asbury, Jo-Ellen. "African-American Women in Violent Relationships," *Violence in the Black Family: Correlates and Consequences.* Robert L. Hampton, ed. Lexington: DC Heath, 1987, pp. 89-105.

Barnes, Edward. "The Black Community as the Source of Positive Self-Concept for Black Children: A Theoretical Perspective," *Black Psychology,* Reginald Jones, ed New York: Harper, 1972, pp. 106-30.

Dubin, S.C. "Symbolic Slavery: Black Representations on Popular Culture," *Social Problems,* Vol. 34, April 1987, pp. 122-40.

Karenga, Maulana. "Social Ethics and the Black Family: An Alternative Analysis, *The Black Scholar,* Sept./Oct. 1986, pp. 41-54.

Ladner, Joyce, "Black Teenage Pregnancy: A Challenge for Educators," *Journal of Negro Education,* Vol. 56, Winter 1987, pp. 53-63.

_____. "Black Women Face the Twenty-first Century: Major Issues and Problems," *The Black Scholar,* Sept./Oct. 1986, pp. 12-9.

_____. "Intergenerational Teenage Motherhood: Some Preliminary Findings," *SAGE: A Scholarly Journal on Black Women,* Vol. 1, 1984, pp. 22-6.

Nobles, Wade. "Africanity: Its Role in Black Families," *The Black Family: Essays and Studies,* Robert Staples, ed Belmont: Wadsworth, 1978, pp. 19-26.